HOW TO DO A STEW

A Man-guide on: How to Date a Stewardess
By Dr. Lee, "Fly-chiatrist"

For all those who have loved, still love, want to love,
or think you would really love, to be a Stewardess...
this book's for you!

First published by Dog Ear Publishing
4010 W. 86th Street, Ste H
Indianapolis, IN 46268
www.dogearpublishing.net

ISBN: 978-145750-661-1

This book is printed on acid-free paper.

This book is a work of a creative imagination and a hope for a better future. Although some historical information is included, the author was not born at that time deeming it "hearsay." Names, characters, circumstances or situations are purely fictional and any resemblance to any person, living or deceased is coincidental. No animals were injured as a result of this book.

Printed in the United States of America

Contents

Part IV The Final Approach

Dedication

My intent in writing this book is to acknowledge the tens of thousands of hard working Fly Girls and Boys in the world; past, present and future who have missed more than one Christmas dinner or family celebration in order to tend to needs and foster care to that of total strangers. I tip my hat to the Super Stews who dedicate their lives daily to fighting fires, saving lives and kicking tail … with a smile.

Acknowledgements

I would like to give thanks to my many friends, old and new, who helped bring a scrambling of thoughts and a quagmire of scribbles to life. To those who gave encouragement, constructive criticism and invaluable advice; to those who took time to share their stories, thoughts and insights.

There are a host of people who contributed to this work in more ways than they will ever realize. I want to particularly thank Bonnie Trenga, my editor, for the assemblance and red ink. Buck Jones, the greatest talent and cartoon illustrator, who brought my characters to life and put the delicious frosting on the cake. I give special thanks to my good friends, Gina Fergen, Linda Velazquez, Amy Walsh-Mantzey, Lora Lockert, Lenny Rosenburg, Dennis Hackin and Andrew Too for their positive energy and great conversation.

I want to give special thanks to my mother and father for teaching me to enjoy the simple things in life; to stand up for my beliefs; to always lend a helping hand to someone or something less fortunate and first and foremost, be true to myself.

And last but not least, I would like to thank my beacon of light, Jonathan Read, aka "Edward Scissorhands", for that most memorable day when he shredded, chopped and mulched my very first manuscript; endured "the wrath of Lee"; left the scene of the crime, only to return to show tenacious strength and dedication of untold amounts of time, in helping me resurrect and launch "Project Stew." I am thankful for his corroboration and support; for giving time when he didn't have time to give; for nudging me out of my nest and encouraging me to fly solo.

Intro:

Pandora's Box has finally been opened, and years and years of hidden secrets are now flying out for the entire world to hear! *How to Do a Stew* is a step-by-step personal playbook that gives men a "heads up" and a peek at the inside world of a sexy profession filled with a commodity of untamed, fancy-free women who fly, otherwise known as "The Stewardess!" Available in print for the first time are the basic tools to make your "Fantasy Dream Stew" come true! So stop drooling boys, it's time to get in the game. This man-guide is full of humorous tips and tactics, to dos, and taboos that will give any guy, shy or not, the confidence to land his own "Susie Stew"—not just ring her bell! Discover insider information and secrets on how to get a date, be a great mate, and perhaps permanently land a girl with wings!

Full of priceless enlightenment and banter, *How to Do a Stew* is a direct flight to a lifetime of exciting vacations, benefits, and more nuts than you could ever imagine! Written with men in mind, this lighthearted read has something for everyone and anyone curious for a panoramic peek at what really goes on behind the drawn curtains and through the minds of the girls that say, "B'ah Bye!"

Better get your reservations now, before you hear the recording, "Sorry boys, all flights are full!"

Part I

Welcome, I'm Bored;
Your Flight Crew Today Will Be ... Complicated

Attention, All Stew Lovers

Men love Stews. Every man that I've ever met, anyway. And if you happen to be one of these meat-lovin' men, or a vegan for that matter, then this may be your lucky day. This little book could possibly change the rest of your life—and you don't even have to attend church this Sunday or endure a chapter a day for the next 40 days.

Not to worry. It's not to educate the male species on how to conquer the kitchen or cook to impress a newfound love. It's not the hot new, all-organic recipe for a deliciously tender rump roast, cooked at 325 degrees for 2.5 hours, served with red-vine tomatoes and a medley of colorful vegetables swimming in a wonderful Bordelaise sauce accompanied by a bold, beautiful, full-bodied red wine. And you won't have to purchase any gidgets or gadgets, or speak to a foreigner from a land far, far away by dialing my 800 number and pressing 1 for English or 2 for Spanish. Seriously, this is better.

This is a simple guy-guide for those who are tired of striking out in the game of love; filled with defensive moves and clever strategies that'll enable even the slightest of men a grand slam home run! It's fresh and hot and "fun-damental." It's your own personal playbook, that finally gives you men a "heads up" and a sneak peek at the inside world of a sexy profession filled with a commodity of untamed, fancy-free women that fly! She is the top female athlete of the airline industry, known in the inner circle as the "running back," spending most of her time running back and forth delivering non-stop service, as the crowds watch from the sidelines. She's the frisky little flying filly that oh-so-many-men

4

have dreamed about lassoing for years. She is the "Fantasy Stew," there to make all your dreams come true. The girl with the wild mane and swishing tail, trotting up and down the aisles; the one men long to take home, toss on a saddle, and attempt to stay on for that 10-second ride of their life. The real men: chomping at the bit to turn up the heat in the kitchen and try something new and exciting!

More specifically, it's a *How to Do a Stew* cookbook that's, well, overdue, written for men but with women in mind. A particular, intriguing kind of woman … one with wings! I've filled this book with something I know a lot about, and—believe me—it's not cooking. Ask my boyfriend; I can burn a boiling egg. So, I'm sticking to what I know best: Stewardesses.

The following pages are chock-full of secret ingredients and mouth-watering morsels I've been accumulating for over a quarter of a century. They've been simmering on the back burner, waiting for just the right moment. And, fellas, that right moment is now. Every hungry man's appetite, whether young or old, will be fully satisfied and yearning for more. Consider this book your very own "Complete Idiot's Guide to Dating a Stewardess," written especially to enhance the relationships between men and that super sexy group of women, lusted over from afar, known as "Stewardesses."

You'll know exactly what to do and what's taboo when you approach a girl that can fly! These chapters include everything you'll need to know about how to catch, and keep, the saucy little Stew that spends a majority of her life 35,000 feet in the air juggling beer and nuts. And by nuts, I mean passengers. No offense.

This campy little book is my candid opinion, with a primary focus on tips and tactics that will give men the confidence to land their own Susie Stew, not just ring her bell. Discover insider information and well-preserved secrets on how to get a date, be a great mate, and perhaps permanently land your very own Stewardess. Find out how and why the life and style of a girl with wings is uncommonly different from the life and style of anyone you've ever met before. Follow my advice, and you'll attain:

✔ How to prepare yourself for the proper approach and how to land a first date

✔ What makes her tick and, more importantly, what ticks her off

✔ What's fact and what's fantasy in the life of a girl that can fly

✔ How to become "Mr. Right for Good," not just "Mr. Right for a While"

For better or worse, with lots of takeoffs and turbulence but hopefully no crash landings; whether a quick fling or the real thing, the faster you learn your plays, the better your chance of landing one of the rare, highly sought after and close to extinction "Fly Girls."

Serving up privy propaganda and juicy gossip, *How to Do a Stew* is non-stop bevy of knowledge and direct line to a world of infinite great fun and entertainment. If you're ready for your fantasies to come true, buckle up tight boys and prepare for the ride of your life!

"What's a Stew To Do?"

Fantasy Stew

Sit back. Relax. Fantasize. Let your imagination run wild ... I did. As a farm girl, I grew up fantasizing that the profession of a Stewardess was one to be respected, admired, and coveted. A Stewardess was an iconic figure, not unlike a police officer or a firefighter: an honorable position in life. She was a person held in high regard, one with a 20-year retirement.

When I first began my dream career, I had visions and high hopes, to say the least. Soaring way above the billowing clouds, I was to embark on a profession that my mother and father would most certainly be proud of. Needless to say, they would receive keen benefits as well: free flights, non-stop nuts, and plenty of stories to share. My dream was about to come true.

But first, there was arduous work to be done. I had to earn my wings. The weeks and weeks of training were intense and grueling, to say the least. My class was filled with 47 bright, shining, attentive faces eager for their futures to unfold. Our days were spent memorizing page after page of federal rules and regulations, safety and security measures, first aid, emergency evacuation drills, and rigid company by-laws. Nights were spent isolated in sterile hotel rooms, cramming and creating inventive ways to store all this new information, while sipping a late night junkie's cocktail of black coffee and NoDoz.

It became apparent early on: fighting fires; saving lives; wearing the correct color of nail polish, lipstick, and blush—all were of equal importance. A large part of our training consisted of memorizing first aid measures word for word (ands, ifs, and buts included) and practicing land and water evacuation drills while screaming commands in synchronization over and over until hoarse. We were bound to rigid make-up, hair, and grooming styles and given daily approval or disapproval by our peers on personal appearance from head to toe throughout the training program. More color on our cheeks, more hairspray, more polish … more, more, more than this farm girl could ever apply. It was clear that saving lives and looking good were the utmost important factors if one desired to become a perfect Stew.

Upon graduation, 41 other rookies and I passed all final inspections; we were awarded a set of wings, our very own personal identification badge, and a nametag to display proudly. We were all hot to trot; to broaden our horizons and join the ranks of the proud that flew.

With my chin up, my shoulders back, and a shiny new nametag, I was now one step closer to becoming a "Fantasy Stew," rubbing elbows with Sean Connery, serving caviar and the finest bubbling champagne, all the while chatting it up in a sleek airplane filled with rich Howard Hughes types: handsome, single men. The life of a Bond Girl was just one flight away. It was the perfect job for me, a "007 Sky Goddess." Exotic world travel surrounded by wealthy, sophisticated men, while adorned in designer wear and white-fitted-gloves was not just a dream after all. Finally, this farm girl's fantasy was about to take flight.

I could not have been more naïve. I quickly came out of my REM state while working my very first flight to… Midland-Odessa, Texas. It was 6:13 on a Friday night when I realized that my daily duties with this particular low-cost carrier consisted mainly of passing out nuts to nuts, along with serving free-flowing, unlimited amounts of beer and boxed wine, followed by a bit of cheap entertaining. Not too long after, I figured out that the cheap entertainment… was me.

Singing, dancing, and juggling, while sporting a half-baked runway smile, were just a few of the nightly acts I was expected to perform. My dance routine came naturally, as I tripped and stumbled over large bags and body parts overflowing into the aisle while I juggled a tray of drinks on one arm and tossed nuts to a packed house with the other. Throughout my circus performance, I was often urged to sing a funny song or two, but when the day ended, I sang only the blues, wondering, "What in the #@!* did I get myself into?"

I wasn't alone wallowing in self-doubt; most of my classmates were in the same state of shock and confusion. I kept asking myself and the man upstairs, "Why me, Lord?" I kept hoping that the host of the 1975 television series "Candid Camera" would suddenly appear from behind a partition and shout, "Smile, you're on Candid Camera!" I kept hearing the word "Smile, Smile, Smile" throughout the day and throughout the night. It echoed in my dreams. Where was Allen Funt? I kept looking for the hidden cameras while hoping someone would just pinch me.

Well, Mr. Funt never showed up, and I'm fairly certain he is past his retirement age. Boy, how time flies when you're having a good time. I now find myself looking for Demi's cutie-pie husband, Ashton, to come running around the corner to deliver a big surprise hug and yell, "Gir'l, you've been Pun'ked!" As of today, neither man has appeared, yet somehow I still keep searching for the cloud with a silver lining. And every so often, I wake up in a cold sweat, dreaming of Ashton.

After my first few weeks as a Super Stew, it became painfully obvious that my dream bubble had a few holes. I began to correlate my new life experience to the 1980 movie "Private Benjamin," where Goldie Hawn played the part of a naïve, sheltered woman who got duped into joining the army by appealing ad campaigns. The recruiter had made it sound as if the military were full of glamorous world travel and life adventure. As for me,

I fell hook, line, and sinker for the television advertisements for this super low-cost carrier. They portrayed the job of a Stewardess as non-stop fun! Well, the job was non-stop all right, but I certainly didn't consider it fun. Not my idea of fun, anyway. My job as a Stewardess had absolutely nothing to do with fun, nor did it have a retirement. I felt I had been terribly misled. Like Goldie's character, I felt duped.

My definition of fun was soaking up some rays on a tropical beach, snorkeling with friends, and sipping on an ice-cold margarita delivered by a cute little cabana boy with a little cabana tan. That's fun. But there wasn't any sandy beach at the end of my day, nor was there room for a blender, let alone a tan cabana boy, in my little 3' x 4' cracker box of a kitchen called a galley.

I found myself in a very precarious position, and for the first time in my life, I questioned my thoughts and actions. Was my dream job nothing more than just another paycheck, and, more importantly, might my old job still be available? Prior to my Stew-ship, I'd worked with a small scuba diving agency teaching dive classes. After completing the course, the entire class would fly to Cozumel or the Grand Cayman Islands for certification. Crystal clear blue water filled with tropical fish by day, lobster Thermidor and ice-cold margaritas by night. And yes, there were plenty of tan cabana boys. Alas, I'd found that great jobs don't last, so I spent night after night racking my brain and wondering, "What's a Stew to do?"

Several classmates gave up the good life early on, but I didn't consider myself a quitter—or maybe it was that I didn't want to face my biggest childhood fear, telling my parents. What would they tell all their friends back home? How could they survive without free travel benefits? They were already hooked on free flights, and I was the one responsible for their addiction. I was their supplier. Taking their benefits away cold turkey would be cruel, and the thought of having a quitter for a daughter—well, that was all too much for this Stew to stand.

Sure, there were options—there always are—but I chose to keep my dignity, endure the pain and agony, and simply believe that God must have a bigger, better plan for me. Why else would this be happening? I was a good girl, and I wasn't about to fall from grace. So, from that point on, on every single overnight, I did what every good girl does: I prayed and I prayed and I prayed. When my prayers weren't answered (the lines must have been lit up with all the other Stews trying to connect), I decided to go the Deepak Chopra route and give it up to the universe. I let the laws of nature take their course, and I poured myself a glass of chilled wine.

After months and months of treading in a sea of libations, I was finally willing to accept my fate. I stopped second-guessing why the Lord was too busy to answer my 911 call when I realized "No answer was the answer." The fog lifted, and the message came in loud and clear. I was to stay right where I was and "wing it." What a relief to know that I didn't have to scroll through another Sunday paper and graze the classifieds in search of yet another exciting, non-stop fun opportunity. Looking back, I think the reality of it was that I was just too "plane tired" to do much of anything else. My life was exhausting.

The next several months crept by like a snail inching its way across the runway of life. Senior crew members gave constant assurance that "the fly life" would improve dramatically once I made it through the probationary period, so I licked my wounds with a dash of salt and tequila to bide my time. I found myself in a semi-delirious state, comparing my situation to that of a rookie baseball player working his way up the farm league ladder before he hits the Big Leagues, or a sorority pledge going through hell week—only, this hell week lasted six long months. But, evidently, I had to pay my dues if I was ever to say goodbye to the tarnished gates of probation hell and say hello to the pearly gates of seniority heaven. So, I took what little hope I had left and prepared to endure the hazy forecast that lay ahead. I took a deep breath, applied the daily war paint, and took my place on the front lines.

Finally, six months passed. I'd made it through my probation period without any broken bones, just a few aches and pains and a much-bruised ego. I was now considered a full-on employee, and a union member to boot. Sadly, on my first day as full-fledged Stew, after six months and one day, nothing much changed. No bells, no whistles, no celebration band waiting for me—just the same emergency ding dongs demanding emergency beer and nuts, and the same obnoxious whistles and night howls that continued to echo throughout the narrow metal chamber that contained me.

My Stew do-dies were more like those of a beer babe at the corner bar than those of a professional career girl proficient at fighting fires and saving lives. I found that my regimen consisted of tossing cocktails to the left, cocktails to the right, cocktails, cocktails all through the night. I was learning first hand why some people associate a Stewardess with a "glorified waitress in the sky." (Believe me, that was *not* the job I signed up for, and there was most certainly no glory involved.) The flights were filled to the brim with cowboys, cowgirls, and all-you-can-drink free cocktails and chaos. Both front and back galleys were standing room only because they were simply closer to the bar. Turbulence or not, there were 122 thirsty party goers aboard a cabin filled with billowing cigar and cigarette smoke (surely, many of you remember those crazy days when over half the cabin was lit up), and it was clear they had needs and desires the size of Texas to be met.

Beyond the non-stop service was the non-stop hours of delays spent in airports and on active runways … waiting … waiting … and more waiting. Day after day, night after night, week after week, quarter after quarter, it was all pretty much the same. I was the new kid on the block, the bottom of the totem pole of seniority. Every other month, I "sat reserve," waiting for the "Bat Phone" to ring. Sitting reserve: That's airline lingo for being on call with bags packed and uniform ready for a last-minute assignment to cover sick calls and irregular operations due to weather and such. If you can imagine what it would be like to be a human pinball in a pinball machine, that's pretty much what reserve is like. Constant chaos. (I don't dare try to explain the madness, so just file it under "fifth date topics" or something, and make sure you have an extra bottle of wine on hand.) The company had to grow and grow and grow some more if I was ever to see a more palatable life or hope to "hold a better line of time." I desperately needed new hires if I was ever to advance from the free booze and barmaid scene.

The months that I was off reserve, I was able to bid for a set work schedule. Since I was a new hire, the only lines I could hold were Thursday through Sunday night. Every night had seven, and sometimes eight, 45- to 50-minute flights with five to ten minutes' of time on the ground between flights. In those few moments the crew performed magic. 122 passengers miraculously disappeared and another 122 reappeared, breaking all industry records. It was as if the crew and passengers had telekinetic powers; they were all working for one common goal: to make this innovative airline fly. As soon as all passengers were boarded, the doors were shut, though passengers were still standing in the aisles with bags in their hands, and engorged luggage bins were still wide open. Trying to get everyone seated before takeoff was like playing musical chairs. Unorthodox perhaps, but it was like a miraculous orchestration of moving particles, and when the music stopped (literally) every person was to be seated and ready for blast off... Ah, the good ol' daze.

The flights were pretty much all the same. Full. Aw-full. Full of two things: people pounding as much alcohol as they possibly could, and smoke. Lots of smoke. After a whirlwind schedule, the best I could hope for was a bed with clean sheets in a hotel that wasn't a 45-minute drive to and from the airport, one that had a good downstairs bar with a live band and a few jovial crews to socialize with to help wind down from a tailspin night.

Most passengers knew what to expect from this new improved flying machine. Cocktails and beer flowed freely day and into the night, and the crews were known across the nation to be saucy, single, and full of song. It was a pioneer airline with cheap-cheap fares, and at that time, most passengers felt they were a part of history in the making. The company's two main goals were to push back from the gate on time, and to arrive at the next city on time. The third—and maybe it was actually equal in importance—was for the passengers to have fun; unfortunately, it quite often came at the crew's expense.

Yet, as fast and furious as the '80s and '90s were, compared to the strict regulations and security that have all but sucked the fun out of the airline industry, I somehow felt safer then than I do now. If there was ever to be a disturbance of any kind in the cabin, I was certain some big ol' John Wayne/Toby Keith-type dude with a Southern drawl would take care of the "situation" for me. Heck, the whole plane would probably break out into a barroom brawl. At least back then, I wouldn't be at the bottom of the pile.

As I reflect back, my life was reminiscent of another favorite movie: "Groundhog Day," where the egocentric weatherman woke up to an alarm every morning at the same exact time, he continued through each day the exact same way, and, oddly enough, the day always ended the same. Nothing ever changed. (By the way, you'll always find a handful, and sometimes a plane full, of those characters on most every flight, especially Monday mornings.) I was living Einstein's definition of insanity: doing the same thing over and over and expecting a different ending to my drama. Over a quarter of a century later, there I was, tripping through each day, just as I had tripped the days before and every day, hoping for a softer landing. Alas, there was very little change: still no Cristal champagne or Beluga caviar, just more beer and demanding nuts.

I finally realized that nothing was going to change unless I became the master of my own destination, because now I find myself a "Seasoned Stew." Perhaps I'm a bit salty at times. After all, I have been "stewing" in my own juices for over 27 years. I am overcooked. Done. Well done, and perhaps burnt just a little bit—but not crusty (not yet). My once-wild mane is now a bit more tamed. My tresses are usually pulled back in a ponytail because it's easy, and—yes—there is a dash of salt and pepper underneath all that color. I thank the man above for good genes, as my thighs are still small enough to saunter up and down the aisles without bouncing off too many shoulders as I pass. However, I am well aware of the fact that fewer and fewer men out there would like to take this little pony home for a ride. A nice long nap is more like it, and somehow I'm OK with that.

So, before somebody decided to put this ol' Stew to sleep for good, I jumped into the Captain's chair and took control. I was ready for a new fantasy; I decided to take charge of my classic, monotone life. This Lil' Pony is taking a different route, before I turn into an Ol' Nag, and my aching bones and body force me to discontinue service—permanently. I'm looking forward to packing my last overnight bag and heading for the big red barn for a little green pasture and R & R. I am finally going to speak my truth. I'm swapping my serving tray for a laptop, and from here on out, I'm going to hang out on a peaceful ranch with my friendly four-legged friends and dish up my saucy secrets to the world. There's no need to pop a slide; that's old school.

To this day, I am thankful that I've not had to save a life nor evacuate an airplane in an icy body of water. But to all of you wondering, I do know how, and it crosses my mind more often than I would like. What I have done is take a refreshing plunge into uncharted waters and redirected my life.

As a pre-parting gift to all my fellow in-flight crew members and to all the people whose lives have been touched by a Stew; to all those who have loved, still love, want to love, or think you would really love to be a Stew, this book's for you.

For those of you still fantasizing and yearning for a "little taste" of what it would be like to date, be a mate, or marry a Stewardess—or, perhaps, if you're "just plane curious"—sit back. Relax. Read on. Let your imagination go; let me help make your fantasy come true. The sky is the limit.

Airhead or Artist?

The route to this book was not straight away, nor was it smooth sailing…

Shortly after I became a Fantasy Stew, I realized I wasn't getting paid to think. It was a real brainteaser. I found myself becoming afraid to think. Thinking I might get in trouble if I continued. Afraid I might lose my job, especially if I said what I was thinking. Not thinking was all very new to me, and I must say it took me a while to accept that it was part of an all-inclusive package. I knew that if I could just somehow master the art of not thinking, it could actually make my life much easier, and maybe, just maybe, my fantasy would come true after all. I simply needed to portray the part of an "airhead," and to do that, I would need to hone my acting skills. Before applying for a Stewardess position, I'd been aware of, and prepared for, the strict airline rules and regulations; I had not been, however, aware of, nor prepared for, the challenging, unspoken "no-thinking part." That would take practice.

In all of my jobs before I worked with the airlines, I had to think. Thinking was always a major part of the job. If I didn't think for myself, I would have been searching for a new job. So, I had assumed that thinking would be a prerequisite for becoming a professional Stewardess. What a surprise. It didn't take long to figure out that the life of a Stew is much more palatable if one doesn't think, and if you can plaster on a smile from ear to ear, without any reason at all, and wear it for your entire day, you're halfway home. It all sounds so elementary, doesn't it?

I now realize that smiling plays a large part in the role of a Stewardess. To a degree, she is paid to stage a smile through migraines and bunions and everyday worries because it makes everyone feel like the world is a happy place. As long as passengers see a smile on their Stewardesses' faces, they feel safe. Whether you're flying through the worst turbulence or finding grounds in your coffee, a smile from your Stewardess lets you know she is there to handle whatever situation may arise. No worries.

At times, I wondered if a transorbital lobotomy would actually simplify my life in the air. I recalled the 1982 movie "Frances," based on a sad but true story, where Jessica Lange played a wildly talented little filly with a mind of her own, but for some reason the people surrounding her wanted to break her free spirit—and eventually they did. Off to the asylum she went for an experiment with tools that looked like chopsticks. That tamed her down all right. After that, her life was super calm in an eerie, aloof, and robotic sort of way. Absolutely nothing bothered her, ever again. True Nirvana. Life was good. (Although, she did lose the love of her life, Sam Shepard, so maybe a lobotomy was not the best route to a great love life.) Nevertheless, she still looked pretty happy, and she didn't seem to have any frown lines at all. After weighing the pros and cons of having to take a medical leave, I decided to stew on it for a while. At age 27, I was still fairly young and wrinkle free, so I decided to put it on the back burner. I felt confident that I could master not thinking without chopstick surgery, and I did want a love life. So I practiced. I practiced and practiced and practiced.

Years later, as I was tossing in bed—alone—late one night, the light went on and I began to think. I had to stop for a moment. It had been years since I'd actually used my brain to do something new and creative. What a rush. It felt so good that I decided to continue. And here I am, opening new neural pathways. I had a business idea, one that could be fun and profitable; one with an exit strategy. At first, I thought about producing a seminar series that anyone who was familiar with or who had an intimate relationship with a Stewardess could attend. They could learn first-hand about the "stressures" (that's my new word; it's a combination of stress and pressure) of a girl that spends a good majority of her life away from home, family, and friends. The seminar would enlighten people as to how a Stewardess's wants, needs, and desires are unique and, more importantly, how to understand, cope with, and maintain a healthy ongoing relationship—with an emphasis on healthy.

Of course, I would need backup and a support team to put on a mock production and role-play with an audience. I imagined my Stew Posse and me putting on funny skits in front of an attentive audience, but corralling my girlfriends on their days off is like herding cats. Then again, there's nothing remotely appealing about standing in front of a room full of guys who have one hand tucked down the front of their pants while they're tilted up on one cheek to cut the cheese in an effort to upstage me. I realize that men would much rather spend their days off in the local bar, plopped in front of an enormous boob tube, munching on beer nuts and washing 'em down with a cold brew-ski or two. What man wouldn't? Besides, none of the girls in my address book would sign up for the humiliation without union scale, and I wasn't about to fly solo.

I admit to having grandiose visions: For the first time, I'd have an audience filled with attentive men watching as I performed my demonstrations in an environment with full-size bathrooms, separate for men and women. And I wouldn't even have to clean and restock the bathrooms when the gig was over. What a perfect world if men who were well behaved, clean shaven, and eager to learn could magically appear. I was quite certain all Stewardesses would line up to sign up their friends and loved ones; it was the eager-to-learn part that was a bit cloudy.

Nonetheless, my idea of a seminar had legs, but it was a short flight to nowhere. Educating the "men masses" seemed like a bright idea at first, but after thinking it through, segment by segment, I recalled one of the great fractured phrases of baseball legend Yogi Berra: "It's déjà vu all over again." Working a crowd was all too reminiscent of my days working on the "dirty bird," doing my rendition of a Stew appearing to enjoy the company of men behaving badly. If there were a bunch of men together in a room with a woman on stage, they would expect to be entertained somehow. I was not about to include a pole in my presentation, so I decided to nix the whole campaign.

There were other options, easier ones. Seminars are very time consuming and costly. And, besides, I'd still have to shower, dress up, leave the house, wear a nametag, and talk for hours to people sitting in cramped rows of little, uncomfortable seats with a coffee and juice set-up in the back. What was I thinking?

As quickly as I tossed my great idea as a producer and director in the entertainment field out the door, another new and improved idea popped into my head—one that would allow me to sleep in and stay up late. No pole required. I would write a book instead. Maybe I didn't have the talent to be a good actress, but maybe I could write. I could stay home and write in my spare time. I wouldn't even have to get dressed, comb my hair, or go on stage. It all made sense. Packing my bags, going on the road, and listening to people tell me to smile 24 hours a day would become things of the past. I would stay home in my pajamas and write.

At first, I must say, I did question my ability to do anything other than fake smiles, toss nuts, and pick up trash. After being a Stew for nearly half of my life, I questioned if I could do much of anything else besides wonder what else I could do. I'd always thought writers lived in cottages overlooking ocean waves that broke onto white sandy beaches, and watched the mist as the fog rolled in. That is, until I saw a popular late-night television show based on a perky girl who lived in a New York City flat and who wrote in her underwear. I could do that. I didn't need an ocean after all, and I always stayed up late. I could fake the perky part; I had years of experience playing that part. This woman wrote about her daily life. I had a daily life. This woman was an actress. I was an actress. Poorly paid in comparison, but still, I did act. And I had underwear … somewhere.

I would write my memoirs. For over 25 years of my life, I'd played the role of "Dr. Lee, Fly-chiatrist," listening to the sultry love stories and broken hearts of women idolized by many and understood by few. I was the keeper of a vault that held more than a quarter century of love stories gone bad. My rather large shoulder pads helped to soak up their tears, but these lonely hearts needed more than a good shoulder to cry on. They needed someone to go to their homes and tell their boyfriends, family, and loved ones exactly what they needed and explain why on earth they weren't the same happy-go-lucky people that walked out the front door just days before. They needed someone to explain how emotionally exhausting it is to pack up and leave home, day after day, night after night, and year after year and wait on hundreds and hundreds of strangers with special needs. They needed someone who could rant and rave, and squawk like a Banshee hen with her head cut off, if that's what it took to get their point across. They needed a "stand-in," someone fresh to deliver their message, because they were too travel-worn to do a good job themselves. They needed someone like a Denny Crane on that great American legal drama, "Boston Legal"; no, they needed the other one, Alan Shore, to represent them and formally present their case. They needed a David E. Kelley to write their script. Then again, the perfect choice would be a combination Lawyer/Stewardess, someone that knew firsthand what the real life of a Stewardess was all about and who also had the strength and character to build a great defense.

Time was of the essence, and with a budget of zero, the quickest and most cost-effective way for the Stew society to get their just representation was for one of "them" to simply play the bad guy—to become "The Be'ach" (The B.I.T.C._.)! This group desperately needed a "sponsor," and that was a tough role to fill.

Having studied psychology, coupled with my own personal experiences, I am well aware that ranting and raving is a great way to ruin any relationship. It's also a great way to ruin your day. I've done it, but I did it too late. I held in my emotions like a good Stew is taught to do; I bit my lip and tried to please everyone, at work and at home. I learned to be the peacekeeper and put my personal needs on hold. Lots of women do it. Few of us like to come home and let off steam at a loved one, so we bottle it up and bottle it up and cork it, until one day, the bottle explodes. It backfires. By then, it's too late; we have suppressed so many little issues that sometimes it's just easier to pack our bags and go. (Yes, we pack again.) I was tired of packing my bags, and I was equally tired of playing the role of the good girl. I knew that if I put my mind to it, I could play the "B" part, but I would not go on stage; I would use a book as my medium.

There was no time to waste. It was time to find *my* underwear. It was time to unlock the door and share the secret sauces of the traveling Stewardess and sponsor my girls. I wasn't 100% certain that I could be a good writer; then again, I did take English 101 back in my college days. I could do this, and maybe I didn't need to be a great writer. If the guy who wrote that *Little Pieces* book could do it, I could too. What kind of professional background did he have, except for being a professional "baloney" salesman? Didn't he make most of that stuff up? I wouldn't have to make anything up. My story was the real deal, and I knew that thousands of people across the world could relate. Anyway, I was too spent to make stuff up. I just needed to muster up the energy to write down my thoughts and remedies, change a few names, assemble everything to some degree, and call in a few favors from friends.

It was time to change direction. Time to face that four-letter word: fear. I would compile all my years of experience and novel ideas and put them in black and white. I'd finally take the comic's mike and do something fun and worthwhile. Nothing would make me happier than to put a little sunshine back into the lives of a most wonderful group of most deserving people: Stews and their families, friends, and people who love them. Heck, maybe this book will even bring back a little more glamour to the industry. Who knows?

All I knew was that I was willing to take a chance. I couldn't toss nuts to nuts all my life, could I? That image alone was enough to hurl me into the next galaxy. It was time for me to get out my laptop, before it was 5 o'clock somewhere. The time to write was now, before the arthritis set in, or before I checked myself into a bona fide nuthouse.

I quickly opened my laptop and sat with my best friend, Miss Chardonnay, in preparation to write my first sentence. My brain was ready to begin, but evidently my fingers were still thinking. There was tapping, but there was no typing. The tapping just made me more nervous. I was trying hard to be clever and creative. I tried so hard it hurt. I still wasn't quite used to thinking again, so it took some time. I tried again and again. I thought that maybe scratching my head would work. So I scratched ... and scratched ... and scratched. Scratching worked on TV, but still nothing. I was drawing a blank screen, like the one that used to come on at midnight, back in the '60s, when the television stations went off the air. (Maybe I'm dating myself...)

But anyway, there I was, thinking, "Thinking is tougher than I remembered." I thought that maybe a pot of black coffee would get things moving. It had worked in college. Well, a thick black cup of Joe got something moving all right, and as soon as I returned from the bathroom, it came to me. Something was missing; it was my thinking cap, and now I had to try to remember where I had put that little cap. I would really have to think about this one. I never throw anything away. (I got that from my mother.) I needed a search dog, like one they have at airports, one that could save me a few hours, sniff through the house, and find it for me. So much for wishing...

After seven hours of serious digging through layers of old boxes and cluttered drawers, I found it, covered with thick fuzzy stuff. It had been way up high with the other hidden treasures resting under my Rottweiler Ike's chewed-up dog dish from 1994; God rest his soul. Evidently, I hadn't used my thinking cap for a really, really long time—about 25 years. But as soon as I saw it, I knew there was hope. Soon after methodically placing my cap on my head, I began to think.

My first thought was that I needed a little help with faking the perky part, but once I remembered the ol' trick to the Miss Universe pageantry smile, I was on my way. I strolled to the medicine cabinet and, to my surprise, found a slightly used jar of Vaseline. For those of you who have ever wondered how the pageant girls keep their smile on ... well, I'll let you in on a little secret: A slather of Vaseline on the inside of the upper lip will do the trick every time, come rain or shine! I had my thinking cap, the fog was lifting, and I had a perfectly chilled glass of Chardonnay. My smile was from ear to ear, and I even found a pretty, new pair of underwear! Now, I was ready to write.

Hostess History

Before we start swimming in the pool of single Stews without our life vests, let's take a quick trip down memory lane and do a quick Stew review.

From what research I have gathered, air travel in the early 1920s was just slightly better than crossing the country in a covered wagon. Although airplanes were a great means to deliver the mail, which is still a great source of income for carriers these days, the aircraft exteriors were very thin skinned; the smell of fuel fumes filled the cramped cabin; the ride was anything but comfortable and was definitely not for the weak of stomach, but more for the adventurous, frontier thrill seeker. Most people chose to travel by ship or train over air for both comfort and safety reasons, as not only were early commercial airplanes deafening to the ear, but passengers often endured cancelled flights and last-minute mechanical problems.

In 1922, German and English airlines began hiring teenage boys to assist with flights; these "cabin boys" were the very first attendants. European airlines took a more regal approach by recruiting professional adult males from first-class hotels, ocean liners, and top-notch restaurants, thus attracting a more sophisticated group of travelers. "Stewards" then entered the airline world, and the evolution began. The "aerial courier" took the first American flight in 1926, and by the end of the decade, the trend continued as airlines around the world began to employ professional men to serve gourmet meals, assist passengers during flight, and perform a host of other details such as handling baggage and doing paperwork.

Air travel was becoming more alluring and was poised to take off when the stock market crashed in 1929, causing cutbacks with the airlines and leaving the couriers unemployed. Shortly after came Charles Lindbergh's historic transatlantic flight, and the industry gained new life. In 1930, Boeing hired the first registered nurses, who added polish to a very tarnished industry and who brought with them a sense of safety mixed with a hint of sex and intrigue. And thus, the first Stewardesses took flight. Beyond ensuring the safety of the travelers, they also added that feminine touch, making passengers feel more at home and personally cared for. A true "Hostess with the mostess."

During World War II, nurses began enlisting in the armed forces, which led the industry to open its doors to the general public, giving it yet another opportunity to change its image. The airline industry was about to get a face lift, and fortunes were to be made by placing provocative beauty queens and charming young women on a different kind of front line. Thousands of single, white, attractive females who had never dreamed of leaving behind their secretarial chairs, dish-pan hands, and mundane careers lined up to prove themselves worthy of as posh a position as a professional Stewardess. The few that were lucky enough to make it into class found themselves mandated to wearing high heels, make-up, nylons, and girdles and to following a strict weight regimen. In the '50s, *Life* magazine declared the Stewardess "The Glamour Girl." Many airlines hired single women only, and it was known up front that they were working under the "Catch and Release Rule." (You catch a man, you get released!) Some married secretly, choosing to hide their wedding rings, and some succeeded … until the uniform didn't quite fit the way it was intended. When the baby bump began to show, it was a sure sign that there was something in the oven other than salmon or filet mignon. The single girl's sex appeal was a great marketing tool, and airline executives cashed in … as long as they were allowed.

During the revolution of the '60s, sex continued to fill the air, and with the help of the 1964 Civil Rights Act, discrimination of race, religion, age, and gender flew out the door, which added a new dimension. In the early '70s men—straight and gay—pried the doors open as they fought and won the right to work in a predominantly female industry. The cabin crew menu was adding new dishes daily, and there was now quite an assorted platter to choose from. This led to yet another name change in the profession. The glamour girl industry, once dominated by fabulous, voluptuous women, was evolving once again, and a more professional, non-gender-specific title, "Flight Attendant," came about. Both males and females were sharing the same cabin, and now even mothers could apply. Women were allowed to fly if they were married; they could wear glasses; they could add a few pounds and throw away their box of Clairol hair color. The rigid rules and appearance standards were beginning to loosen up as the nation became less uptight and more "all right." In the '60s and '70s, hot pants and fashion boots appeared on the scene; the flight crews became the epitome of sexy boy toys in the sky. But in the '80s and '90s, "hip was hot," and the sky turned to wrinkle-free polyester pantsuits, manty-hose, and frump.

My first intimate relationship as a Stewardess was with another Stewardess, a man Stewardess. When I was in Las Vegas on an overnight, I was shopping for a pair of panty hose to replace the pair I had ruined earlier that day. (Back then, we were mandated to carry an additional pair of panty hose in our travel bag in case of a snag or run.) I was dating Michael, and we were flying together on a three-day trip. Since males and females were supposed to be treated equally, I thought it only right for him to wear a pair as well … so I bought him his first pair of manty-hose. For those who can't imagine what they might be, they're panty hose with a third leg. Ingenious … and warm, I've been told.

Today, while some airlines still follow a manicured look for their cabin crew, many have taken on a more casual, non-gender-specific, public look. Designer heels were replaced with Sketchers sneakers and comfy clogs, and if it weren't for the set of wings worn by the cabin crew, in many cases it would be difficult to tell passengers from crew members. Caviar was replaced with crackers, and nowadays the Domino's delivery guy sitting in row 4C and helping pass out nuts could easily be mistakenly for one of the crew members on many low-cost carriers.

Boy, how times have changed.

I was hired in the early '80s by an airline whose flight attendants were predominantly female. Although other airlines had been hiring men since back in the '60s, this particular airline built its empire on pretty women with big hair, hot pants and Go Go boots. As the years flew by, more and more men began appearing alongside the fun loving and spirited cabin showgirls. The hot pants were replaced by a more unisex uniform, but big hair still ruled. The cockpit was full of testosterone, but working next to these new men—who were handsome, flirty, charming, and full of life—brought a new dimension to the cabin. Having hard bodies on board certainly added an interesting ambiance; it also meant the possibility of one more man on the dance floor. The cabin began to look more like Barbie and Ken's playhouse, and I must say, all the girls I knew enjoyed having a man around the house to help lift heavy bags and show off their bulging muscles if a passenger dared step out of line.

Hotel accommodations were company paid, and after a late night, it wasn't uncommon for a barf bag filled with cans of ice cold beer to appear suddenly on the long van rides to a cheap hotel. The air was rapidly filling up with more love than one could ever imagine. The most popular hotel lounges offered live entertainment and a 3-2-1 adult beverage menu ($3 cocktails, $2 wine, and $1 beers), which further enticed the cabin and cockpit crews to flock and exchange the day's highlights and top stories that somehow sounded much funnier once retold. Closing the bar down and escorting one another safely to our rooms sometimes left the morning maid with one less room to clean.

Flying with a boyfriend made work more like a holiday, and overnights were bid according to what kind of B & B (bar and band) the hotel provided. That era was the beginning of a blend of attractive men and women with distinct backgrounds and sexual preferences flying under our own "Don't Ask, Don't Tell" flagship.

Seemingly overnight, there was someone for everyone. The air was filling with a smorgasbord of Stews; from tough to tender, thin to full figured, blonde to gray, hot to cold, men to women. These sexy flying machines were no longer required to step onto the scales and weigh in every quarter, nor were they required to have a nursing or college degree. The safety and emergency standards were still rigid, but there was love in the air as the new and improved Stews took on a whole new persona of groovy hip huggers and stacked heels. The cabin oozed sultry, sexy men and women highly trained in verbal judo, zip tie handcuffs, holding hands, and other things, singing and dancing their way across the country and enjoying the high life.

Imagine yourself working in an office where at the end of the day, the entire workforce is bussed to a nearby hotel to spend the night. There is a bar lounge downstairs, filled with like people who have migrated from all over the world to make new friends and rekindle old acquaintances. Men and women enjoy an adult beverage or two—or three—to help them wind down from an exhausting schedule. It is just a matter of time until …. Well, you know the rest of the story. Love happens.

Let's begin when I began working for nuts.

Working for Nuts

Oh, I've spent a great majority of these past years sitting under my sign, "Dr. Lee, Love Jet Fly-chiatrist: I WORK FOR NUTS."

I don't really carry a sign; it's just my little imaginary sign, hung over the incredibly uncomfortable plank called a "jump seat," located in the back galley of a Boeing 737. The jump seat is the special place dedicated for Stews to sit during take-off and landing. It's also where they huddle to gobble down a few bites of a sandwich or to put their feet up for a stolen moment and chill.

Jump seats are not really seats but covered planks perfectly placed right next to the toilet and garbage bins. That's where I collected most of my "data." That's my office. Ironically, it's the perfect kind of dumpsite, where Stewardesses can sit and dump on one another ... in a healthy way. Here, they can dump about the day, the pay, the people, and the home life. They exchange secrets, thoughts, ideas, and hopeful solutions for troubled relationships and oodles of other personal things. Dumping is an important part of a Stew's workday, and the location is ideal. Perfect feng shui: next to the toilet. And, oddly enough, it's also where love connections are made every day.

At the beginning of my career, most flights were well under an hour from gate to gate, leaving little time for Stews to spew or flirt in any shape or fashion. Once the Pilots began to rev the engines for blastoff, passengers would begin to salivate, preparing for their own kind of blastoff (Pavlov's Law of Planes). Cocktails flowed freely, and the cabin was out of control with the excitement of a cheap flight on a new plane, to anywhere. Dallas to

Austin, Austin to San Antonio—it didn't much matter where the plane was going; all flights were jam packed with Texans with a Texas-sized thirst. The "over-wang" exit rows were the hot tickets in the house and were known as the party lounges, as two rows faced one another on both sides, creating a rip-roaring party plane atmosphere for an even dozen good-time Charlies to rock and roll.

The cost of a round-trip ticket was a non-number when it came to partying with the good ol' boys at 35,000 feet, chuggin' as much beer and cocktails as possible, from take-off to landing. Besides, the flying-bar babes were not only young, single, and good looking, but they also had pockets full of nuts, served up with a big ol' Texan "Howdy, Boys" smile ... for a while.

Mindless simple tasks, such as opening sodas, mixing cocktails, and hurling nuts through the air (sometimes one at a time, sometimes handfuls, sometimes the whole plastic bag full), became second nature as the Stews envisioned a moment of rest and an opportunity to "be'ach in the back." It was like holding our own private Flight Attendants Anonymous meeting—in the back galley of an airplane. These were our guidelines:

1. Any information shared was to be kept confidential.

2. Make "I" statements; take responsibility for your emotions.

3. Share what bugs you most at that moment. It could be that you just hyper-extended your back when tripping over another large foot left out into the aisle, your hairdresser gave you a bad haircut, or your new husband just moved into your home with his three children—all under age 13—from his first two wives ... permanently.

4. Give and take advice. Telling someone what to do is refreshing.

5. Cross talk: Ask as many questions as possible, and discuss anything and everything; it doesn't matter if it makes sense or not. Purge and babble.

6. Have an adult beverage as soon as you get home, and chant this mantra: "God grant me the serenity to accept the things I cannot change, the courage to change the things I can, and the wisdom to know the difference."

Our Favorite Motto: "I'll drink to that."

Those were pretty much our support guidelines. We didn't meet once a week; we met seven times a week—day and night, and at all hours—and as rapidly as the company grew across the nation, so grew the membership to our secret sorority. The back galley bench was open 24-7, and it was like a revolving door.

Over the years, the short hauls became longer and longer, as the airline carrier expanded into more and more cities and states. The longer flights gave the crews additional time to exchange intimate details and talk about the nitty gritty stuff. The smut stuff. The stuff you wouldn't dare tell your mother stuff. It also allowed me to develop my real passion as "Dr. Lee, Fly-chiatrist." I have now practiced for over a quarter of a century, with high hopes to receive my honorary doctorate someday, and I could even be in line for a Nobel Peace Prize. I directly and indirectly know the good, bad, and ugly of Stewardesses' relationships. I know what makes them tick—and, more importantly, what ticks them off.

My first year in college, I majored in Psychology. The second year, I promptly modified my major to something more fun and exciting: Parks and Recreation. Playing games outdoors in the sun versus being stymied in a little room where there's a little chair, scribbling notes on a little tablet, while gazing out a little window, listening to people's petty little problems all day long? It was a no-brainer.

Ironically, at the age of 27, I found myself locked up tight in a little room, filled with little chairs, scribbling notes on a little tablet, while gazing out a little window, listening to people's petty little problems all day long. Problems related to the airplane running late; bags being lost; nuts tasting bad; someone stuffing a toxic dirty diaper down the lavatory trap door; and the usual expected everyday travel and in-flight drama. What I didn't expect to find were the endless "love stories gone bad" and relationship woes of nearly every Stewardess, both single and married, and the common denominators they all shared.

The "Sky Bar," the hottest bar around, was filled with single chicks with benefits, and men looking to get lucky. Finding a guy to date was easy; keeping one for any length of time … not so easy. Most girls never found "Mr. Right," but most found "Mr. Right for a While." Many stayed in relationships much longer than they should have, mainly because "training can be draining" for both parties involved. The directions for a sizzling hot, long-lasting relationship with a Stewardess are ever changing. To keep it fresh and salubrious, both cooks need to add their own select ingredients; otherwise, the sizzle turns to fizzle real fast. When you're creating a "Signature Stew," one of the most difficult tasks is getting the main two ingredients into the kitchen at the same time: the cooks.

Over 25 years, I honed my practice and administered advice. All pro bono. Particularly interesting to me were the many similarities shared by this group of women, who leave behind their homes and loved ones to tend to a cornucopia of wants and needs of total strangers. Even more incredible was that upon their return, these same Super Stews never skip a beat. Many strip off the prison blues uniform, tear off the "Oh, Miss" nametag, and drop it off at the front door, replacing it with yet another nametag: "Oh, Mommy." They're like Superman returning to his office as Clark Kent. Now the real job begins.

For those with children or family waiting impatiently at home, there was no stopping off at the local bar for a couple of rounds with the boys. For those with boyfriends or significant others waiting for them, well, most couldn't wait to get home … to an adult … beverage. Cocktail therapy soon became a favorite pastime for my friends and me. The "whine and wine" parties were ongoing events, but they were becoming costly and quite habit forming. Not wanting to spend time in rehab with Paris and

Lindsey listening to them whine about how they hated the color of their Gulfstream's leather interior or not finding their favorite Jimmy Choo shoes on their last New York spending spree, I knew it was time for a change. There was no doubt in my mind; it was high time to get out of "The Nut House." I just needed to figure out the best route and time of departure.

~!~

I have mentioned "nuts" more than just a few times and will continue to do so, so perhaps a bit of an explanation is in order. For those of you that haven't quite figured it out, I work for an airline that built its entire marketing campaign around peanuts.

Little bags of peanuts, the cheapest nuts in the world. Jimmy Carter's roots, the last ones left all by their lonesome, at the very bottom of the bowl of assortment bar nuts after Cocktail Therapy. This ingenious campaign lured customers who identified with, wanted to be, and acted like nuts—the cheap kind. Since I'm an on-board certified doctor of mental disorders, with a lobby full of patients (I mean, plane load of passengers), it seemed the perfect fit and appropriate place and time to ask each individual a closed-ended question: "Nuts? Nuts? You're Nuts?" Yes, it is more of a rhetorical question about their mental condition than their hunger, but it does break up the monotony of handing out nuts to hundreds and hundreds of people a day. Not a thinking gal's game, but an innocent, good-time game. All the same, and believe it or not, every now and then, a passenger looks up from her trance and replies, "Yes, just a bit, but I'm getting help" (probably an ex-Stew).

Stew Defined

Many passengers view the job of a Stewardess as nothing more than a chick paid to hand out stuff like Band-Aids and barf bags, deliver drinks on demand, and take lots of lip service. I can see how passengers might get confused about the real purpose of the cabin crew. Stews do a first class job maintaining a cool, calm, and collected air as they leisurely stroll through the aisles, asking passengers if there is anything else they need and making small talk, like "Oh, what a cute baby" as she wonders how TSA could have missed the Glock-look-alike water gun with which the impudent six-year-old boy in the next row is squirting her face. They are masters of deception, looking more like the girls next door than Super Stews, ready to ward off any evildoers that may intend to harm the aircraft, passengers, or cockpit crew at any given moment.

Let's start with what the real "never-to-be-said-aloud" definition of a Stew is:

A person highly trained to "Save Your Ass, Not Kiss It"

Shocked, right? Not what you normally see a Stew doing. Saving lives, I mean. Just a friendly reminder for all of you not paying attention during the emergency demonstrations: Stewardesses are there primarily for your safety. They're trained to handle every type of emergency on board from a hijacking to a heart attack, as well as to fight fires and defrag a bomb. Every day, they put their own lives on the line, for every Tom, Dick, and Harriet on board. But if the ship is sinking, no matter how badly she'd like to leave behind the jerk that just poked her with his swizzle stick and told her she was fat, she can't. (Then again, nobody really knows how someone under extreme duress will react, do they?) All she and her shipmates can do is wonder how so many passengers can be so insensitive to someone who is *supposed* to save their lives. Believe it or not, people, Stews are *not* there to kiss your keister ... they're there to save it! So, next time you fly, you might think twice about making some derogatory remark or sharing your bad mood with her. Believe me, she more than likely is stifling one or more remarks of her very own.

You're right, though. When has anyone seen a Super Stew fly into action to prepare a "ship load" of hysterical people as they are about to bore a tunnel through a 100-story building, or belly land in the bay? Few have had the experience of watching as she cares for a passenger foaming at the mouth during an epileptic seizure, grabbing the nearest Halon extinguisher to put out a fire, preparing the cabin for a water evacuation, or giving the Heimlich to a pregnant woman or an infant. Very few have been on flights where first aid was administered, and even fewer have been on flights involved in any kind of terrorist attack—and they probably won't know that knitting needles aren't allowed (or are they?).

I've been lucky ... so far. I haven't experienced a death in flight, nor have I had to ward off a terrorist and bean him over the head with a coffee pot, but I have put out my share of fires—daily. During our training, teachers did not cover the on-board passenger fires, nor are they addressed in the pages of my manual. The fires I put out daily are the ones where personalities and conversations get so overheated I'm surprised they don't set off the smoke and fire alarms. Smack, crackle, pop! When you arbitrarily mix the hard-core freakin' flyers with first-time flyers with families, children, and pets—oh, my—and squeeze them all into the same hermetically sealed tube together, the combination can heat up and become nuclear in no time. And it does.

Stewardesses quite often find themselves in precarious positions; never knowing when a gauche situation might suddenly arise. I've had to diplomatically and discreetly move an unaccompanied seven-year-old child who'd been seated next to a lecherous man who smelled like an over ripe chunk of blue cheese; this dude felt that putting his arm around her and kissing the top of her head would somehow make her stop crying. I'm sure he had good intentions; maybe he just missed his own little girl. But on a completely full flight, with all eyes watching; every word said; every move made; is critical.

Sure, I have had my share of hair-raising, scary people on board—people I thought I recognized from the "10 Most Wanted" list and a host of Bin Laden look-alikes—but I made sure to be extra nice: give them an extra pack of peanuts, and try not to look them in the eyes. Who am I to judge? My job is not to profile. My job is to ensure all my passengers get safely from one point to another … and as far as I know, they paid for their ticket just like everyone else. They can't help the way they look, and they probably think I dress funny. Besides, the last thing I want to do on my flight is tick somebody off, especially an escaped convict, and incite a riot. Or, for that matter, get a bad letter in my file.

Much of my day is filled tending to people's needs. I hand out free stuff like Band-Aids to the people with paper cuts; barf bags to the people who are pregnant, ate bad food, or might have cocktail flu; and booze to the people who are celebrating, claustrophobic, or depressed. I hand out an assortment of specialty drinks like a mix of half Diet Sprite and half orange juice, one ice cube or none, and I take lip from everyone and anyone that might have had a bad day and feels the need to share it.

I know of a crew that had to evacuate an airplane that couldn't be stopped within the confines of the airport grounds. It drove right through the wall, crossed the street, and parked directly in front of a gas station, close enough that if the Pilot had been able to roll down the window, he could have ordered a Big Gulp. Sometimes, airplanes have minds of their own; I guess that particular airplane figured that gas was cheaper across the road. Who knows why accidents happen? They just happen. I know only that the crew on that flight put their lives on the line to safely evacuate a planeload of passengers in record time, and that if the airplane had gone much farther either way, it could have easily become an inferno. Hearing stories like that makes me proud to be an affiliate of the Super Stew Society.

Super Stews

Yes, it's understood that the crew's own lives take a backseat to those of every single man, woman, child, cat, and dog on-board. The crew's job is to do their best to ensure every living thing on-board makes it to a safe place in case the landing gears fail, a fire breaks out, or the top peels back and you suddenly find yourself in a Boeing 737 convertible. They're there in case someone decides to light up their shoe, blow up their underpants, or terrorize the people on-board. They're there to make peace with an angry mob-like gang of passengers that have been sitting on a runway for five hours without the use of a lavatory, or access to food and water. They're there in case a baby shoves a salty peanut or an M & M up its nose, a passenger starts foaming at the mouth, or someone flat lines in the aisle. Need I go on?

A major part of a Stewardess's job is to protect all passengers between point A and point B … at all costs. They go through a mental pre-flight checklist of what action to take if a *non compos mentis*(derived from the <u>Latin</u> *non* meaning "not", *compos* meaning "having (command of)", and *mentis* (<u>genitive</u> <u>singular</u> of *mens*), meaning "mind") person suddenly rushes the cockpit, which door and commands they would use if they had to evacuate in a water ditching or landing gear failure, and other secret Stew stuff. They do not pull a suspicious passenger aside just before boarding for a surprise cavity search, nor do they wear billy clubs or stun guns. (Yet.) And no, their title has not changed to "Fright Attendants." (Not yet.) Rather, they are Super Stews/Cape-less Crusaders, flying 35,000 feet through the air without a net, and traveling up to 500 miles an hour as they keep watch over thousands of innocent, unassuming people. They are highly trained on verbal judo and how kicking a guy in his shin will distract him just long enough to allow just enough time to dart through the hysterical crowd; to open a secret compartment; break into a bag; remove the plastic zipper cuffs; and return to the scene where the terrorist is patiently waiting for his winsome, five foot two - Susie Stew to wrestle him to the ground with just the right superhero moves so as not to cause him any pain or suffering … as only a Super G.I. Stew is trained to do.

They are expected to put their lives on the line for a planeload of strangers every day, all day, and at the rate the security industry is going, maybe someday, they might just evolve into TSA agents, armed with suspicion and packing ammo. Why not? All terrorist activity that I am aware of happened on the inside of the airplane, right? So wouldn't one think the security agents or Air Marshals should be on-board every flight as well? (Why do *they* get to stay on the ground... where it's safe?) Who's to decide? But at the moment, Stews are your dedicated on-board body guards, waiting patiently for every passenger to board once the security agents have had their way with them. Stews are sweet and kind, mild mannered, mothers and grandmothers. They don't wear Barney Fife badges or dark blue uniforms like prison guards; they certainly wouldn't want to scare anyone. Let's leave that for the TSA. For now.

TSA: Twirl n' Separate Agents

Ironically, the scariest part of every flying adventure these days is what you might encounter at the TSA security checkpoint: men getting their "boys" roughed up and twirled around like a string of worry beads; breast cancer survivors being asked to remove their prosthetic breast to prove it isn't a bomb. (A boob-bomb? Who would have thunk?) What if an agent finds a lump on a woman's breast during the exam? Good grief, what will they do if they find a cluster? And why not offer a mammogram while they're at it? What about all those humongous breast implants floating around out there? (I'll bet there's enough liquid in some of those puppies to blow up the entire fleet!) Most of us have heard about the horrific experience where an 80 year old, dying woman was required to remove her Depends for a brief examination—and while we're talking diapers, what keeps TSA from inspecting the little Lincoln Log in the baby's Pamper? We all know that's explosive material!

Shortly after 9/11, the security scan was turned up so high that an underwire bra would set it off. I thought the whole *purpose of the underwire*—not the TSA—was to "lift and separate." The security boys had a field day with "touching the twins," until too many flights were delayed because female crew members were getting "felt up and freaked out." (As if they'd try to sneak a boobie bomb on-board their own flight.) And the guys were pulled aside to be checked out as to whether they were just born lucky, or just packing their son's toy water pistol. Who wouldn't get somewhat nervous or aroused while being "man-handled" in public with a crowd surveilling from the sidelines?

My friend Brad has been a United States citizen all 55 years of his life. He's a "bionic man" with titanium knees and travels all over the world for business—every week of the year. This poor man gets pulled aside and "patted up down and sideways" *every time* he goes through TSA because of his knees. Sometimes it's a courteous pat-down; sometimes not. (He has never had any trouble in any other country, nor does he have a criminal background.) Tiring of his boys getting twirled around in public (by a man, no less), he recently chose to go through this new and improved "easy-breezy, no more fondling x-ray machine." While standing in front of the all powerful and mighty machine with his hands up above his head, he was approached by two hulky, pan faced TSA agents and told, "We have detected a 'crotch anomaly.' You need to come with us." (Not knowing exactly what a "crotch anomaly" was, his first thought was to call his physician and make an appointment for a checkup.)

To make a long story short, Brad was given the "Full Monty" treatment in a private room for three. "Over the river and through the woods, they went." Just like you see in the movies; the bad ones. No stones were left unturned. Brad called me immediately after the incident. I heard the disgust in his voice as he explained what had just occurred. I had visions of a particular scene in the 1972 movie "Deliverance," with Burt Reynolds. Most of you know which scene I'm talking about: the one with the guys in the forest. (For those of you that haven't seen it and are interested, I suggest you rent the DVD, and *then* you'll know. It's too creepy to put in print.)

As far as the TSA agents were concerned, Brad was guilty of hiding ... something ... drugs ... a "dirty bomb" in his diaper. (Oh no, not again.) Whatever it was, they were bitterly determined to find it. One agent aggressively "foraged" like a kid on an Easter egg hunt, while the other watched. Brad tried to explain that his knees were titanium and that for the first time; he'd chosen the x-ray over the pat-down to avoid this type of treatment and humiliation. Their response was a curt, "You have a crotch anomaly." (Evidently, this world-class x-ray picked up on something in Brad's pants that couldn't possibly be of human form. After the intense investigation, they found he wasn't hiding anything; the package was all Brad. He was guilty of nothing but being born lucky. This type of story is something Tim Allen could run hog wild with. It's easy to make jokes about—if it didn't happen to you.

So, I guess the "immoral" of the story is if any of you men know or think you might have a "crotch anomaly" or have future plans to have one, do *not* go through the x-ray machine. Take your chances. A private pat-down is intensely thorough, and in this situation the TSA's actions and behavior were absolutely uncalled for.

If you have nothing better to do someday, Google "crotch anomaly." You might be surprised how many other stories just like Brad's are out there.

Sadly, these types of stories are everyday occurrences, and even the children are involved in the pat-downs. People, what about "Stranger Danger"? How can parents be expected to hold their screaming, terrified child as a stranger puts their hands all over his or her tiny tot body? What kinds of nightmares are our children going to have? Does anyone know how it will affect them as adults? Maybe it's time to start thinking about it before we become so desensitized that nothing shocks us anymore!

As of this writing, all carry-on liquids must be in containers 3 ounces or less, (no, the 8-oz. tube of toothpaste can't have only a squirt or two remaining), fit comfortably in a clear, quart sized zip-top bag, and separated from the rest of your carry-on while you go through the security checkpoint. Oh, and be sure to remove your shoes, belt, watch, coat, paper clips, nipple ring, or anything else that may set off the alarm. Oh, and be sure to keep your arms close to your body. If they get too close to the walls of the people scanner, it will set off an alarm and you'll have to retrace your steps and try again. Or, if you are just plane ol' lucky (there will be no profiling!), you'll be patted down or escorted to the holding pen and "wanded" with the security guy's joystick! Oh, newsflash: "NO MORE WANDING"; again... old school!

I'll bet the wand stock price dropped to 0 … unless the company had a corner on the latex market as well! (And you know it did!)

One thing is for sure: The policies of airline travel and the security rules and regulations are ever changing. Just when you've run out of clever complaints and don't think twice about the 97-year-old man and his wife getting fondled and frisked because they are wheelchair bound, wear pacemakers, and have titanium hips and implants, the security turns it up a notch, and another layer of rules is imposed on the meek, the weak, and the innocent. The wands disappear, and now TSA lets their latex-protected fingers do the walking … over every inch of the passengers' bodies. (I can only hope the thousands of bags, boxes, and shiploads of cargo get checked so thoroughly.) How exciting to know TSA has created thousands more jobs since 9/11 and to know there are government jobs available where workers can actually get paid to grope men, women, and children in public, and they have retirement packages!

My friends, those are some of the things that frighten me in this new-and-improved, false-sense-of-security airline industry, and crews must adapt and comply with the modifications daily. What next? Check the poor little therapy dog to make sure his master didn't tape a stick of dyno'mite to his little unit? How sad for Sparky.

Whether road warriors or holiday travelers, most passengers understand firsthand the demands and fatigue that accompany life on the road. Air travel can be nerve racking and stressful no matter how well thought out the plan, no matter how thorough the checklist. Once you leave home, the variables out of your control are infinite. By the time you read this book, I'm most certain the rules and regulations will have changed—yet again—so there's no need to go into every minute detail. The simple rule of thumb is this: The only thing constant in the airline world is change. It's just a fact; expect the unexpected. The more experienced the traveler, the easier the task should be, but that's not necessarily true. It's very much the same when you're dating a

Stewardess. The more minutia and meat and potatoes you can amass and digest about her lifestyle and profession ahead of time, the easier it should be to make sense of her ever-changing moods. But just as every airline, every airport, every travel experience is authentic, so is every Stewardess.

Mystery Stew

Over the years, many people have asked me and/or my crew members what it's like to be a Stewardess. In all fairness, it is a different job every day. Some good, some bad, some ugly. Some days, I'd rather have a root canal without the Novocain; other days, it is smooth sailing and gives me just enough hope that maybe tomorrow's flights will go without a hitch; that all passengers will someday say please and thank you; and that not everyone will wear "juicy" printed across their low-riding, sloppy pink sweat pants that drag on the ground and that show off their "whale tails," "muffin tops," and "tramp stamps."

Most Stews I know make a point to find something or someone on the airplane that makes them laugh, or something—anything—to help them get through their day. Me, I'm a dreamer. I have hope. I know it's just a matter of time till Snooki and her cast of "Jersey Shore" reality royalty will parade on-board as the next crew, and they'll bring back some funk and fun to an industry that has all but flat lined. Now, that's what I'm talkin' about. That'll really bring the glamour back to the industry. Until then, I hope you will enjoy my view of the mystery of the Stew 2011.

"What's it like to be a Stewardess?" Let me take the mystery out of the meat once and for all. Then, you can tell two friends, and they can tell two friends, and so on, and so on, and soon, all the energetic, hopeful, hardworking girls, boys, men, and women around the world will have a better grasp of what it's really like to be a Stewardess. Then, someday, I hope in my lifetime, everyone will know what is fact and what is fiction, and I won't have to be the one to break the fantasy bubble or take the rap for having a bad attitude. I am not a "Debbie Downer," I am a "Raelene Realistic." I'd like the public to have an undisguised, realistic view of the job; it's not all "glitz and glam."

The crowd doesn't go wild with cheers and applause when the new crew takes over; it's not like when Lakers coach Phil Jackson sends in Kobe Bryant to take over for Steve Blake in the second half of the game. Heck, we can hardly get the people to move out of the aisle so that we can put our luggage bags up and check emergency equipment before the flight; that's how noticed we are.

Very few people are intrigued about the jobs of carpenters, mechanics, accountants, or secretaries. Most everyone knows what those particular jobs entail, but for whatever reason, there is a real enigma surrounding the Stewardess. Maybe it's that over the years, television and movies have portrayed the life of a Stewardess as glamorous and free to travel about the country without a care in the world; what could a Stewardess possibly have to grumble and moan about?

Or maybe it's because part of the "job performance" is to work through the pain of migraines, lack of sleep, no union breaks for meals, and such, while trying to masquerade it's a perfect world. Advertisements show Stewardesses smiling from ear to ear with really clean, pressed uniforms, eager to greet really cheerful, well-dressed passengers, with one carry-on bag each. They appear in the cabin loaded with a host of beverages and an enthusiastic smile, but no one sees what goes on behind the drawn curtain. No one sees the coffee pot overflow and leak into the ice drawers, down into her socks, and onto the floor. No one sees the soda can explode in her face, the cola spraying her hair and staining her clothes as the tab grazes her forehead. No one sees her as she as turns into a contortionist trying to fit into her Barbie doll-size travel kitchen, so she can squat and crouch and tug on heavy beer kits crammed into compartments much too small, while simultaneously tearing her rotator cuff and splitting a fingernail as she comes up and hits her head on the corner of a flying cabinet … again. No one sees how many people ask for a bite of her squished peanut butter and jelly sandwich as she attempts to eat breakfast, lunch, or dinner on a hard plank attached to the wall of a "very well traveled" flying Porta-Potty. Yes, we get grumpy too; our legs hurt, our veins pop, our nerves are shot, our skin and hair are dry, and we fly with two permanent carry-on bags—one under each eye—and you already know where we dine. Some days, I come home with so many bumps and bruises, I feel like Rodney King. Top that.

At a dinner party, when I am forced to confess, "I fly," a deluge of questions and atrocious travel stories fills the air, and I find myself surrounded by strangers starving for answers, like a rat on a Cheeto. Taking the blame for lost luggage or late flights is not how I want to spend my evenings out. I try to politely divert the conversation to another topic, but somehow I always end up getting grilled and losing my patience in an attempt not only to defend myself, but also champion for the entire airline industry.

Passengers only see Susie Stew cruising the cabin, sporting smiles, serving up beverages and catering to a potpourri of needs. They have no idea how many flights the crew has already flown; how many flights they have ahead of them; what time of the wee morning they left the hotel; or how badly their backs, legs, and feet hurt. Stews pretend to lend a sympathetic ear to those who dare complain about having to make one, two, three and four stops from New York to Los Angeles. People, try working it!

Passengers don't realize that when they are late, Stews are late too, but somehow the conversation always comes full circle to what a great life and utopic job it must be. I admit that yes, there are certainly advantages to being a Stewardess, but the job also has its unique disadvantages, it can be quite taxing mentally and physically, and the industry is like no other. On my days off, rather than talk shop, I personally would prefer to discuss my golf game and the kind of kitty litter I buy.

So, for those of you who think you know what it's like to be a Stew, I have a little exercise drill for you:

Close your eyes, clear your head, and use your imagination. Envision yourself at the nearest shopping mall. You blindly choose 137 people. Invite them to your home and greet each one individually as they enter your front door. Let them know that the seating arrangements are—just like at the movies—first come, first serve. Make sure all seats are super-close to one another, so the people can hardly move. Leave barely enough room for an aisle way, so you can feel like the "Bing-Bing-Bing" of the great Hanna-Barbera cartoon Ricochet Rabbit, deflecting huge shoulders, thighs, and kneecaps as you attempt to deliver service with an engaging smile. Give them each a bell, so they may ring you with whatever question or need they may have during their stay. Strap them in—elbow to elbow, knee to knee. Once you are certain they are all individually properly seated and secured, ask them to turn off all their cell phones, game boys, and any electronic devices they have brought to your home. Next, walk past each row and politely ask whoever is still using a headset to take it off, and then—again—request that the rest of the guests who still have their phones and laptops and all the other gadgets on to turn them off. Get prepared for these individuals to give you a look of disgust as if you are nothing more than a nuisance as they continue to text and hide. Good luck with that. Once you have reprimanded them again and again for not turning off all their ADD toys, walk to the front door and lock it. No, my friend, not as you leave; you are locked on the inside, with them. No one is allowed to open a window for fresh air; no one is allowed to leave for any reason whatsoever. Ever. You now have a captive audience, and the games are about to begin! It's now time to play "Freakin' Hostess for the Day!" The entire freakin' day.

Let's start with the easy stuff. First, watch them ignore you as they sneak their headsets back on during your emergency demonstrations. Wait for about 15 minutes—just enough time for some to fall asleep, some to start their own movies, some to start reading their paperback or electronic book or to work on their laptop, and the rest to lose their patience because they are thirsty and waiting with nothing better to do. The next step is to try to submissively interrupt each one of them so you can ask what they would like to drink, and then you wait patiently to collect the coupons, credit cards, or debit cards as they retrieve them from their pockets, purses and carry-on luggage. Don't forget about the guy two rows back; he was snoring just seconds before, but now he's tugging your shirt because he needs a beer (to match the six-pack he probably had for breakfast with his mini-Cinnabons in the airport bar). You find yourself saying things like, "No, we do not have champagne" and "No, I can't take that diaper or sloshing air sickness bag just now." You say, "So sorry, folks, but we don't serve food," while thinking to yourself, "I think we had to get rid of the pillows and blankets because of head lice or swine flu or some kind of health hazard, or was it because we needed the space for all the elephant-size bags?" You deflect a hodgepodge of questions, saying, "Sorry, I'm taking beverage orders at this time, but as soon as I get everyone served, I'll be right back."

Go to the smallest space in the house (say, your coat closet), mix the drinks, and deliver them, all in 10 minutes before an earthquake shakes the neighborhood and you have to rush to grab a seat in the closet before falling down. Once the house stops shaking, look around and cautiously try to stand up again. Peek around the corner, only to find that everyone in the house is now paying attention; all eyes are on you (tomato juice stains and all), trying to read your facial expressions and eye movements, waiting and watching to see just what your next move will be. (Is she bleeding, or is that just Clamato?) Everyone is feeding off you. You savor this moment in some demented kind of way thinking: "Now, I have their respect." And then…

Oh no, someone has rung his emergency bell. If you rush out, is it worth taking the chance that you'll get hurt yourself? Of course! You are a superhero, so you take your life into your own hands. You rush like the legendary Jim Brown to address the emergency call, only to be told, "You forgot my nuts." After you apologize that the seat belt sign is on and explain that it isn't safe for *anyone* to be up, return to your "time out" chair before you say something you might get suspended for. (Then again, if you plan your calendar right, a few days off over Christmas might be nice.) When it's safe, you nonchalantly clean up all the spills, wear your warrior stains as if you weren't even aware of them, and tend to all the crying babies ... the adult ones. Never fear, "Super Stew is here!" (And don't forget the nuts.)

To get a true sense of the job, make sure you have enough toilet paper, hand soap and paper towels, because you're also on Potty Patrol! Oh, and be sure to have plenty of fragrant "air spray" to cover the "egg and chorizo burrito whiff" that will be hovering in your home. Try placing a mini- chair just outside your bathroom. That's where you will be eating breakfast, lunch, and dinner. M' m', good!

And be prepared for a barrage of "Simple Simon" questions throughout your day:

- ✔ Why are you late?
- ✔ Where is my seat?
- ✔ Is my bag on-board?
- ✔ Where are we?
- ✔ What time is it?
- ✔ How long is the flight?
- ✔ What do you have to drink?
- ✔ What are you serving for lunch?
- ✔ Why don't you serve food?
- ✔ Where are the pillows and blankets?
- ✔ Why aren't there pillows and blankets?
- ✔ Is the restroom empty?
- ✔ What's the weather like?
- ✔ When do we get there?
- ✔ What are all those green circles on the ground?
- ✔ Why can't I use my cell phone?

✔ Is my mother on-board?

✔ Do you have any toothpaste or gum?

✔ How about a fork?

✔ What gate are we coming into?

✔ What gate will my next flight be going out of?

✔ Will my wheelchair be waiting?

✔ Do you know my cousin Tim?

✔ What's it like to be a Stewardess?

✔ Can you get me a pass?

✔ Why do you look tired?

✔ Why aren't you smiling?

✔ What's *your* name? (the most dreaded question of all)

When your exciting day is done, you'll stand at the front door and tell all your guests the famous "B'uh Bye," in a way that only the "Saturday Night Live" crew could capture the translation of this emotionless send-off. Once they're gone, you get to play hide n' seek, cleaning up the house and checking inside drawers and under furniture to collect whatever mysterious remnants of smelly food your guests have hidden for you to find. You'll also get to pick up other gross indescribable "gifts," such as used tissue, broken ink pens, gooey Gummies, cookie crumbles, oil stained bags of half-eaten food, and an assortment of unwanted paraphernalia left behind. Oh, and don't forget to be on high alert for any improperly disposed medical needles. They've treated your home office no better than they would a movie theater (not that trashing a movie theater is acceptable, either). Rule of thumb: It's just like camping, kids: "You haul it in; you haul it out." I'm guessing passengers don't realize that the same fingers and hands that pick up these begrimed items, also dip into ice drawers and serve drinks throughout the day and night. Not that you won't have time to wash your hands. I'm just saying.

But wait, it's better yet, for within a few minutes of bidding the last passenger adieu, you'll have a whole new set of 137 strangers at your door, and they'll be loaded with bags and baby strollers, food, therapy pets, trash, troubles, and "tudes." You'll get to repeat your performance—perhaps up to six more times that day.

Welcome to my world. Then, when your final hour is over and you think you can finally relax and kick off your shoes, a surprise guest comes knocking at your door. You're about to be invited to a private after-hours party. Drink up. What follows is a true story.

The Pea Party

Random testing for drugs and alcohol was unheard of back in the early '80s. The only random drug testing that occurred back then was done in the "on-site lavatories" (commonly known as the "back lab" by a few stoner passengers flying just a little bit higher than the rest of the crowd, due to a little enhancement that came in a little brown vial or paper wrap).

Fast forward to 2011, when drug testing is now a part of everyday life for the cabin crew. Nowadays, when you least expect it, you are personally invited and chaperoned to an after-hours work party. I christen it the private "Pea Party." It's more like a surprise party for one ... of the lucky Stewardesses at the end of her day, or night; it could happen at any time of day or night. It doesn't happen every time, and I've been told it is in fact a random drawing; that there isn't any real method to the madness. Who knows? All I know is that it is always a surprise, but not a nice surprise, and it happens when you least expect it. It happens when you forgot about the possibility of this social soiree, and right before landing you used the restroom so you wouldn't have to stop at a Circle K after midnight on your way home. It happens when you have plans after your flight, like catching a close connection to meet a new love, or simply needing to go home and catch up on your beauty rest after a grueling day.

It's quite humiliating as an adult to have to try to remember not to use the bathroom on the last flight, for fear of being met by a strange person in a dirty jetway with a clipboard in hand. This person has only one thing on his/her mind. This person, who is waiting just outside the aircraft door, is there to personally escort you to a special place where you get to blindly aim and tinkle in a small plastic cup the size of a shot glass. The "Pea Inspector" accompanies you to the bowels of the airport, watches you wash your hands, gives you the special cup with a line on it, shows you to the restroom door, and says, "Be sure not to flush." No plastic gloves and no other details than that.

The last time I was invited to this private party, it literally took me just under three hours to complete the task. I failed miserably at my first endeavor. My chaperone suggested I drink some water, so, hoping to produce a gusher, I guzzled nearly half a gallon. Still nothing, except for the fact that I was now waterlogged and woozy. As I lay on the filthy carpet, pushing on my poochy tummy while watching a late-night documentary about how the Panama Canal was built, I started hallucinating about the prisoners who are kept hostage at Guantanamo Bay and found myself feeling compassion for them. I was under severe pea pressure, held hostage in the basement of an empty airport by a man I didn't know. Finally, at 2:28 a.m., just shy of three hours after I'd first tried, my water broke and I gave birth to my very own Panama Canal. The Pea Party was finally over and I was good to go.

Susie Sky Cop

Yes, due to heightened security standards and the ways of the world, sex, drugs, and rock and roll rolled right out of the airline industry. Taking "morning hits" off the oxygen bottle to rid ourselves of hangovers from last night's cocktail flu came to a screeching halt overnight. The hip and happy industry once known for sexy slogans such as "Come Fly Me" and "Just Say When" slowly turned into a tattered and tired industry on high alert that at any given moment, another tower might turn to ash. These days, maybe a more appropriate slogan might be "Just Plane Tired" or perhaps "Just Say Why."

Planes are no longer filled with well-dressed Prince Charmings sporting coats, silk ties and tips. Nowadays, although the airplanes do carry their own "on-board ties," they unfortunately are not the kind of ties worn with tailored shirts. The new and improved ties are stowed in a secret Stew compartment and used only when necessary to handcuff and apprehend a possible terrorist or anyone that appears to threaten the aircraft or passengers. Make sure not to yell, "Hi, Jack" to a friend you suddenly recognize on-board, or you may find yourself face down with your nose stuck in some chewed-up gum and being handcuffed by a sweet and unassuming "Susie Sky Cop"!

Yes, the poised, polished, and impeccably coiffed Hostess, once uniformed with delicate, white gloves and a stylish pill hat and serving heavenly canapés and bubbly champagne, has traded down for a pair of powdered latex gloves and a set of plastic zipper cuffs. The dainty gloves that once fitted the dainty hands now come in a cardboard box—small, medium, and large. These particular gloves are not for serving a delightful meal on a delightful tray on a delightful day. They have multiple uses, and there is nothing delightful about them.

If you listen closely to the "galley gab," you will be certain to hear mumbling such as "This isn't the job I signed up for," or "I think the freak in F4 just wiped a booger on me." Over the past 75 years, her titles have changed from Hostess to Stewardess to Flight Attendant to Oh, Miss to Hey, you, just to name a few, and as her titles have changed, so have her lifestyle and attitude, both in the air and on the ground.

She now guards the cockpit with her life and knows how to fight off a psycho terrorist by gouging out his close set beady eyes with her two fingers, take him to his dirty knees with verbal judo, and turn a mere swizzle stick into a deadly weapon. She can only hope the Scuzz-ball has a swizzle stick less sharp and shorter than hers. She knows how to precisely handcuff an unruly passenger, making sure the cuffs are not too tight or too loose. As in the story "Goldilocks and the Three Bears," they'll be "just right." She trusts no one, not even the half-blind lady (or is she?) who accidentally (or is it?) pulls on the cockpit door, thinking it leads to the lavatory. No one can really be trusted, not even her fellow crew. She can't even really trust herself, for who knows what sneaky Pete might have slipped into her back pocket while she stood in line for her holiday peppermint cocoa.

A Stew will not tolerate any jokes about security, sex, or her hair-do; rather, she'll take immediate action. She is the incognito "Susie Sky Cop," serving sodas, snacks and cocktails while making lilliputian small-talk to everyone on-board. These same people could very well be the enemy. Who else is there? Think about it.

P.M.S. - **P**assenger **M**ental **S**train

PMS: Passenger Mental Strain

Every Stew I know suffers from PMS: Passenger Mental Strain. Here are the top three PMS home remedies for relief:

1. Sleep alone.

2. Drink alone.

3. Drink with her Stewardess friends.

I personally like to drink alone, because I don't have to talk to anyone. Except my cat, and my cat does not talk back. My first cat talked back. I had to give her to my mother and get a new cat, one that didn't talk back. She is my therapy cat. It was either Prozac or a cat. I chose the cat. I named her "Prozac."

Plane Nuts and More

It's simply Pavlov's Law of Nuts. One person rings his emergency call button, and everyone on the airplane hears a bell. Game on. Someone is getting a reward. They all watch like hawks to see who rang their bell and what kind of prize the Stewardess is going to retrieve for them. It's just a matter of time until another passenger "E.T." finger goes up in the air and searches for a place to land. All too many believe that when they press a button, a genie in a bottle containing pockets full of nuts and goodies will magically appear. A seasoned Stew will drop whatever she is doing and sprint to reach the call, before another nut button goes off. Or, on second thought, she might just peek around the partition to see whether or not the crowd has their "Eek, it's a real emergency" face on, and at that point she'll make a more educated decision about whether to walk, run, or finish her can of lukewarm chili con carne.

If a Stewardess deems the crowd is wearing their "eek" face, she instantly turns into Super Stew, flying through the air, twisting, turning, and leaping like a gazelle over anything that may at any given second appear in front of her and perhaps impede the saving of a life. Alas, upon reaching the illuminated call button, she finds not a passenger in need of the Heimlich but one that needs round of Heinekens for himself and his "eek"-faced friends.

As she returns with arms loaded with beer for the boys, out of the corner of her eye she sees yet another semi-comatose passenger's "E.T." finger slowly creeping up to find his call button. (Or is he just looking for the light?) She is once again in emergency mode, trying to stop the madness of the "ding-dong game" before it gets out of control and an avalanche of emergency nut buttons rings through the cabin, alerting everyone that a Super Stew is in the area and that she just might be packing pretzels and nuts.

For those of you who are not just reading, but absorbing as well, yes, the little airline known for "nuts" has pretzels too. I'm not sure who decided to put pretzels on-board (probably the little person behind the curtain again). Everyone seemed happy with peanuts, until they were given a choice. And now that I've told the rest of the world that they have a choice, I'll have to try to remember to stuff a package of pretzels in my other pocket for that one out of 250 people that needs a pretzel.

Me, I love peanuts. I don't know what I would do without them. They are the perfect passenger pacifier. I never had children, but now I understand why parents attach binkies to their children's clothes. As soon as the baby cries, mom or dad puts the binkie in. Peanuts are like binkies. I love them. I don't know why we have peanuts and pretzels. You don't see parents carrying two types of binkies, do you?

Besides, pretzels are different from peanuts. Pretzels land on the floor more often than peanuts. Maybe they taste stale, so people throw them on the floor. I don't know. What I do know about pretzels is they get crushed into itty-bitty pieces—pieces so small, they are nearly impossible to pick up off the floor. I realize it is not the passengers' fault. The packaging is so incredibly difficult to open that once they have managed to tear the pretzel bag apart, the pretzels go flying. Oops, there they go: onto the neighbor; between the legs onto the floor; under the feet; under the shoes, crushed into tiny particles of dried flour, water, and salt. Little pretzel parcels left for the maid—I mean, the Stewardess—to bend over and pick up.

I think it's fun for men to watch Stews bending over. Maybe it has something to do with seeing them wearing little gloves and crawling on the floor? I have yet to figure it out. But I do think that just like the simple man portrayed by Peter Sellers in one of my favorite movies, "Being There," a lot of men are voyeurs.

Chance the Gardener liked to watch. At least he admitted it; heck, he was proud of it. Men on the airplane watch, but they don't like anyone to know they're watching. I watch them watching the Stews, as we stretch over our heads to rearrange all the oversized luggage left in the overhead bins and bend over to clean up the "dirty bird" after every flight. (Note, however, that we have been strongly advised not to use the phrase "clean up." A more professional word like "tidy," as in Tidy Bowl, is evidently a more appropriate choice.)

By the way, if, as the plane is descending, you do hear a Stew announcing that it's time to "clean up" instead of "tidy up," this means there is a rebel on the loose. This bad girl could possibly have a Harley Davidson parked in her garage. So, heads up, boys; this one may have some spunk left after a long day on her feet. She might need to lie down as soon as she gets home, and maybe, just maybe, not alone! Keep a close watch on this one. She just may color outside the lines.

Crop Dusting

WARNING!

THE FOLLOWING CONTAINS HAZMAT MATERIAL.

FOR THOSE WHO CHOOSE TO READ BEYOND THIS POINT, YOU HAVE BEEN PRE-WARNED. YOU MAY NEVER LOOK AT A STEWARDESS IN THE SAME WAY.

IF YOU ARE ON AN AIRPLANE AS YOU ARE READING THIS,

WE HIGHLY RECOMMEND YOU EAT BEFORE YOU READ.

Now that everyone is aware of the additional snack choice, another tidbit of information is about to seep out—no pun intended! Some may find it in poor taste; others may think it worth the price of the book. Me, I'm just the messenger.

One day not too long ago, my mother asked me, "What do you think when you see a Flight Attendant who's not smiling?" My answer: "She has a good reason. She likely has more than several." And all these reasons have been bottled up and brewing inside—some for a moment, others for years. Then again, if she is smiling, buyer beware. Something in the pot may be stirring. Here is a little secret about smiling Stews: The plane goes up, the body expands, varicose veins bulge, feet and ankles swell, and before long ankles morph into "cankles." Cankles are ankles so large they look more like the calves on a sumo wrestler than the ankles of a petite, sweet little Stewardess.

As if those issues weren't enough to deal with, the worst little issue of all is trapped gas. I know, I know. It's not a comfortable subject to talk about (especially for girls), but this "subject" can be not only uncomfortable but also very painful in reality. Then again, a little "good ol' gal gas" can be fun. Seriously, it can't be helped. Cramping leads to wrinkles, which is the real reason a Stew needs to let "little fluffy fly." A lady cannot excuse herself and step outside, nor would she step into a lavatory (too much competition), leaving only one other option: the center aisle, a perfect place for "crop dusting." Sometimes, Stews "dust" with a smile, sometimes with a poker face. There is absolutely no way to track a Stew; she glides up and down her little private runway.

So, to all the little pests who mock her during her emergency demonstrations; to all who ignore her; to all who have been rude and obnoxious; to those who have been asked time and time again to put their bags away and turn off their toys; to the ones that drink too much, talk too loudly, and toss their trash on the floor; to the ones who have earned their "Freakin' Flyer" wings, be prepared for a surprise Stew flyby. Many men have probably been "dusted" and weren't even aware it was happening. Taking the blame was the big, hulky guy sitting in the row ahead of you and eating the Whammy's Big Boy Cheese Burger with a couple sides of jalapeño nachos and deep fried onion rings. Surely, it wasn't that sweet little Soufflé who just whizzed past.

The girl with the sincere little grin plastered from ear to ear most certainly has a way of making a silent statement (though in a rather passive-aggressive manner) by using some good ol' home-brewed pesticide to dust those who intentionally bug her!

No device on Earth can be certain where her haunting little gift came from. Maybe it's time for two of my favorite ghosts of the past, Aykroyd and Murray, to bring out the guns for "Dust Busters"! (We all know Sigourney would make the perfect alien Stew.) Till then, enjoy, all you passengers behaving badly, and welcome to In-Flight Pest Control!

So beware, my good friends, of the "Smiling Stewardess"; she might be up to no good!

Detox

While we're on the repellent subject of dusting, let's talk about detox.

Stews clean up after hundreds of people daily: Some are straight out of the hospital, some are on their way there, and some don't even have time for a checkup. In fact, those that pre-board quite often look like the walking wounded or wheelchair-bound patients from the E.R. And, of course, the cabin is filled with hacking, sneezing, and recycled air.

Stews, therefore, absolutely must find a way to detox, or, in other words, get the gunk off. A Stew literally has been breathing infectious air and collecting germ-ridden trash, bad attitudes, and travel drama for days at a time, and it is essential to purge; otherwise, she may turn into a human trash collector and someday even a rotten Stew. And nobody likes a rotten Stew, not even her mother.

It's not easy to purge. She can't put her finger down her throat in the back lavatory or hit the trash or delete button and eliminate her varied gunk collection. Being a member of Flight Attendants Anonymous, a Sister Stew knows she can call another member 24-7 for an emergency spew, but she's also aware that she must be prepared to listen in return to her sister's spew and sometimes … well, sometimes, it's just easier to tap into a nice, cold Chardonnay.

Non-airline family and friends don't want to listen to her daily regurgitation of in-flight drama, and that's most certainly understandable. The constant delays and continuous petty problems get old real fast … for everyone. Yet, it's still imperative for her to find a way to clear herself of the stressful pressures and toxic materials she inhaled and absorbed throughout her day.

Detoxing for a Stewardess is a decompression for the mind, body, and soul. It's an essential part of her life. It's not that she is hiding a "secret little problem" (the company has an 800 number for that); her problem is very well known. A Stew needs to decompress for several reasons. One serious reason is that her immune system is constantly compromised by fighting off toxins and germs, which are unfortunately a part of her everyday work environment. Another reason, and perhaps the more obvious, is that since stepping foot on-board the aircraft, she has been passing out "nuts to nuts," and the nuts have simply worn off onto her!

Every Stew has her own specific way of detoxing. Here are a few favorites:

✔ Letting off a few rounds at the shooting range

✔ An afternoon of Archery

✔ Locking herself in her room and watching "One Flew Over the Cuckoo's Nest"

✔ Meeting with her psychologist

✔ Using lots of swear words

✔ Unplugging all phones

✔ Going to the gym

✔ Picking weeds or gardening

✔ Chopping wood

✔ Taxidermy

✔ Painting

✔ Running her fingernails down a chalkboard

✔ Playing with her voodoo dolls

✔ Cleaning closets (this is one reason you don't want to be around: she may just be in the mood to toss things out, and if you're in the way, you might just be one of them)

✔ Taking an Epsom Salts bath with a few drops of lavender (the salts help draw out toxins that a body absorbs on airplanes, from metal to mold to cleaning products to, well, lots of funky stuff)

✔ Going on a shopping spree, buying tons of cute clothes, and not paying any attention to the price, knowing that in the next couple of days she will be returning them (it was a feel-good adrenaline high for a while)

✔ Going to the pharmacy for a refill on her prescriptions

✔ Self-medicating with alcohol (the #1 quick pick)

Part II

Let's Get to the Real Meat of the Matter

Fly Girls

A key factor to having grounded, rounded, lasting relationships is to read about Fly Girls, their jobs, and their lifestyles both at home and in the air; understanding and implementing this information is yet another. Their wants, needs, and desires change like the weather, and strangely enough, the weather often plays a major role in their daily lives and attitudes.

Both Stewardesses and the concept of travel are alluring, sexy, and infatuating; they can also be unpredictable and stressful. No matter how many questions you inquire about an airport, parking, baggage, security checks, boarding, deplaning, and flying in general, you can never be overly prepared or have too much information. Every airline, every airport, every terminal, and every off-site parking lot is completely different from the next, and all change daily. Passengers must make reservations in advance in order to receive a decent fare, and they must print boarding passes at home in order to save time and get a decent seat on the airplane. It's difficult for even a seasoned traveler to keep in the know.

Packing simply has become an art within itself. You wonder what clothes to take and try your best to coordinate colors and ensembles; you must pack lightly enough so you don't get charged an additional fee; and as you set your bag on the scale at the ticket counter, you cross your fingers as you wonder what it's going to weigh. If you're under your max, you wish you had brought an extra shirt or two and if you're over, you wish you had left that unnecessary pair of shoes behind. Some airlines charge for any bag that is checked and/or brought aboard, no matter its weight or size. To this day, it amazes me that so much space is allotted for baggage. Where I grew up, we had wonderful basements in our homes that were great for indoor "rough housing", as my mother used to say. The way the economy is today, maybe future air travel will offer "Basement Fares" where the passengers could bring their own fold up chairs and do whatever the heck they want during the flight. No seatbelts – no Stews – no supervision. What a great place for cage fighting. Now that's what I would call in-flight entertainment! A kind of "BYOC" - bring your own chair, kind of fare. Outdoor events have the super cheap seats where you bring your own chair, right? If it works on the ground...why wouldn't it work in the air? When times get tough... Corporate gets creative. It could happen.

It's just a fact; expect the unexpected. The more experience the traveler has, the easier the task should be. It's very much the same when dating a Stewardess. The more detailed information you can gather and learn ahead of time about her lifestyle and profession, the easier it will be to understand her ever-changing moods. But just as every airline, every airport, and every travel experience is unique, so is every Stewardess. And ever changing at that.

The Dating Game
Bachelorette #1, #2, or #3

If after reading thus far, you still have an appetite to date, mate with, or in any way relate to one of these magnificent flying machines, you may be one of the few to figure out the Rubik's Cube of the puzzling Stewardess relationship. An important piece of the puzzle that will help you to create the perfect match is finding which Stew's right for you. They come in a variety of shapes and sizes: hot, medium, and cold. For starters, try to figure out which of the following bachelorettes is perfectly seasoned and tempered just right for you.

Behind Door #1: The Hot Stew

The Hot Stew is steamy and has a tendency to overheat easily. She talks fast and saunters slowly through the center aisle in her tightly-fitted, highly-starched uniform, checking to ensure all seatbelts are strapped tight and low. Imagine her wearing a monocle and swastika as she inspects that all tray tables are up and locked and that all iPods, uPods, blueberries, Black Berries, raspberries, and any electronic devices are in their off position! It's a perfect time to exercise her female domination, and she hopes to reprimand both CEO and redneck alike, thereby proving her Super Stew powers.

Watch out, boys. This one may be high maintenance and is definitely a control freak! If you should ever peek into her closet, you may find it filled with black leather ensembles, stiletto heels, and a crop whip or two. Used. She may fly off the handle and lose her cool, but you … naughty boy … made her do it. Her temperature runs at the boiling point, and she is on high alert at all times; she's ready to pull the lever and take command of any given situation. She is fast moving, quick to take action, and somehow alluring to most men with a weakness for being spanked. Get her home (or meet her in her hotel room) with a couple of cocktails, and the hair comes down, the garters get unsnapped, and the heels are kicked across the room … at you! Love her or hate her, she runs on high octane.

Fellas, be sure to wear your oven mittens (or bring your own leather gloves) when romancing a Hot Stew; like it or not, you may get burned!

Look, I'm smiling and I don't even know why!

Behind Door #2: The Medium Stew

The Medium Stew is even tempered and a favorite to all. Not too hot, not too cold … just right! I would guess that most Stews fall into this category. Her mild manners and easygoing temperament are pleasing to many, and she just might be the one you bring home to mother. The girl/wife next door, she's a multi-tasking, full-scheduled, family and friend kind of gal, who could probably make time for the right guy. Whether or not her easy-breezy personality is enhanced by her prescription pal, or she was just born with lucky genes, the Medium Stew has somehow learned not to let all the "Ding Dongs" and cabin nuts get to her. Men, you won't have to wait for this one to heat up or cool down, but you might want to sneak a peek-a-boo into her medicine cabinet before planning your first overnight.

She's seemingly a great catch, but keep an eye on her; if her meds aren't just right, you might find her serving packaged peanuts as hors d'oeuvres at your next cocktail party, handing out drinks in familiar plastic cups, and giving boarding announcements to guests with her former cheerleader's megaphone. Sweet and simple as she may appear, she may be one flight away from becoming a Stepford Stew.

The Medium Stew comes with a "Buyer Beware" sign, but there are no gloves required with this mild-mannered Stew!

Behind Door #3: The Cold Stew

There is something about a Cold Stew. Aloof and challenging, this particular Stew is for the more experienced player who knows the importance of a good warm-up before the big game. Be sure to crack your knuckles, boys, or she may just crack 'em for you. She is quick witted, is independent to a fault, and has a guaranteed slam-dunk comeback for every line known to mankind. Don't dare tell this one to smile, or you may hear her whisper in your ear, "If you were handsome, honey, I would already be smiling," followed by a quick wink and a sweet little smirk broadcast from ear to ear for all to see. She is a clever one; she's always on "high-smart-ass alert" and is ready to field any half witted comment thrown at her. The wink of a seasoned Stew is just a diversion to throw a man off course, and to let him know she's a pro and has the home-field advantage. This is her turf. The passengers on the sidelines might think she is flirting with you. Take it from someone who knows firsthand—she's not.

It takes the right kind of man to tenderize this Stew. A man that is patient, smart, and kind hearted—and that knows when to shut up. Boys, do not attempt to outsmart a Cold Stew; she is for an experienced cook only. She may take a tad bit more time to unthaw, but she may also be well worth the wait. In the game of love, as in any sport, the warm-up is essential. So, for those of you willing to take the time to pre-heat, slow cook, and open a good bottle of cabernet, you may just find a best friend and perhaps the love of your life.

Take time to warm her up appropriately; otherwise, be prepared for frostbite.

Wear kid gloves here.

Rapid Rewards Package

For those lucky enough to land yourself the perfect Stew, you'll eventually learn about her own personalized rapid rewards package. Most people are aware of the non-stop peanuts and a few free passes doled out every now and then, but many, many other rewards are offered to the men that are willing to earn them. Don't get ahead of the game by dreaming of all the free travel to exotic locations the two of you will be taking after your first date. It's getting to that first date that you need to be dreaming of; that alone can be quite challenging, and it's almost an impossible task. The competition is immense.

Whether you've already landed a Fly Girl, or you have intentions to do so in the future, you'll need specific skills, oodles of patience, and serious determination if you're looking for a smooth take-off and landing. Day and night, literally thousands of men are flying around in limbo with their head in the clouds, salivating at the thought of "Doing a Stew." So, boys, stop scratching your head, or whatever it is you're scratching, and get in the game. It's high time to put on your "big-boy bibs" and get ready to drool.

The secrets to dating, mating with, and marrying a girl who flies lie in the pages ahead. Simply follow the step-by-step directions, and pay close attention. There won't be any messy chalkboards, and there won't be any screaming. Well, there might be screaming later in this game of love, but not just now and not by me. Don't worry if you consider yourself a rookie in the kitchen. I'll be your personal chef and will coach you through to a new, exciting, wonderful world of a dating a girl with wings!

Congratulations, Baby, on taking your first step. You now have a confirmed reservation and are one day closer to learning about the real rewards of dating a Stewardess. Once you've learned them, you'll certainly want to know how to earn them, and those, my friends, are the real meat of the matter.

In-Flight Flirting 101

*** Browsers: YOU MUST BUY THIS BOOK in paperback! ***

I know that some guys will probably be browsing around the airport bookstore while waiting for their flight, and they'll be thumbing through this book (because "Penthouse" is in a wrapper), thinking they'll pick up a few tips that will make their trip a flying success. Wrong! It's going to take an investment of time and a little money, boys, but believe me the return will be well worth your while. Half steps result in full failure. You *must* read the *whole* book to understand why. Like a farmer needs his John Deere tractor...you'll need this handy tool to cultivate the perfect romance to land your idyllic Stew.

Finding a Fly Girl is the easy part; flirting with her is an art. Here are some simple steps to help you with both:

1. **Take this guide wherever you go. Own it and flaunt it.**

You may not be aware, but Stewardesses are everywhere, not just in the air. On their days off, you'll find them in grocery stores, coffee shops, pet shops—lots of shops. And there is one shop that they definitely gravitate toward: the nearest wine shop, and you'll find them there chirping about passengers and their love lives, or lack thereof. Literally thousands of Stewardesses flitter about the world incognito, out and about running errands daily, just like the 9 to 5'ers. They may be clean scrubbed, wearing ball caps and sweats while out walking the dog, or dressed to the nines as they go out to meet the girls for whine and cheese at the nearest happy hour.

Many know her as a Super Stew, but she is human too. She does normal everyday stuff like every other girl; it's just harder to identify her if she's not flying through the air. If she's not wearing her wings, you may never look at her twice; she looks like the typical girl next door. Some Stews who have their feet on the ground dig their heels in deep and hibernate like grizzly bears trying to catch up on lost sleep; others move like humming birds at lightning speed, running a marathon of errands on their one day off in preparation for yet another early departure. Yes, they're out there, but the only certain way and a sure shortcut to meet a Stewardess is to make a reservation and board a Love Jet to anywhere.

If you want groceries, you go to the market; if you need office supplies, you go to the office supply store. If you want to meet a Stewardess, go to where all Stewardesses eventually go—the airport. I realize airplane tickets may not be in everyone's budget, but don't give up. You have other options. For those of you saving for a rainy day or too busy to take a vacation, the next best option is to take this book in paperback version wherever you go.

You should take it everywhere. Put it in your briefcase or back pack and take it to work; read it on a subway or while waiting for the light rail. Read it at the corner hangout or while jogging on the treadmill at your local gym. The sooner you begin, the better. You can start slow and read it at your own pace. Pick it up. Put it down. Take your time, but keep it close. Just make sure that people around you see you are reading a book about Stewardesses. Nonchalantly hold up the cover for all to see if you have to.

As soon as you purchase your paperback, brand it like a tattoo. I highly recommend putting your "John Henry" on it somewhere, even if you just picked it up at the airport for a quick read during flight. You'll find out some of the reasons why as you read further.

2. Find a way to get her attention.

Something as simple as eye contact can be the most difficult task. Stewardesses buzz up and down the aisles, and zip through airports as if they are on their way to a fire. (And—who's to say?—maybe they are.) Any kind of eye contact a Stew makes may lead to an unscheduled stop, such as having to retrieve a fifth vodka tonic for a passenger. Eye contact causes her delay, leaving her wide open to a gamut of questions like those you used to ask your mom and dad on that long drive to your grandparents' house: "How much farther?" and "Where are we?"

Passengers get bored very easily, especially if they haven't packed their new Blu-ray disc or DVD player, laptop, iPod, or their newest game-gadget with which to amuse themselves. If a Stewardess is within view, one bored individual, if not more, will attempt to start an "I'm Bored" mind game. It's a kind of on-board target sport that uses verbal quiz-darts (darts the TSA security guards can't take away, unfortunately).

Naturally, the Stewardess plays the moving target. The bored passengers stay seated and throw darted questions until she comes to a complete stop to play the question-and-answer game. This game can go on and on to the point of exhaustion … for her. Now you know why Stews fly by so fast up and down the aisles. Walk fast; make no eye contact. That's body language for "Don't ask." If you think you have a Stew in sight, on or off the airplane, you'll need a bit of a leg up if you are going to attempt to make eye contact or get her attention without sticking a leg out. That, my friends, is one of the reasons reading this book in public is so important. You may have a whole airplane vying for her attention, so be smart and read this book during flight. A tablet type e-book like iNook and Kindle are easy to travel with but the screen page makes it difficult for a Stew to recognize the content. Now, a paperback version, on the other hand, makes it easy. It is a great conversation piece, and if a Stewardess sees you reading a book about her life, believe me, she'll stop for an introduction, and your window of opportunity will fly open. The cover is a show stopper and a vital resource, intentionally designed to get your girl to stop in her tracks. For example, say she comes by to take your beverage order; go ahead and gently close the book with the cover side up for her to see. It's up to you to be prepared for the flirt and play every possible angle. If you are a serious player and have future intentions of having a Fly Girl wrapped in your arms, be sure to keep a paperback version in your hands at all times!

3. Make your friends buy their own paperback book.

Some guys are cheap. Sure paperback books may cost a few more dollars than an e-book, but in this particular case, it's a bargain-priced tool that could easily turn out to be … priceless…if utilized properly. Don't loan this book to your good buddies; you may never see it again and if it is returned, more than likely, pages will be missing. You'll want to have this book intact for future reference and cheap entertainment. Be sure to take it with you while doing things like taking a break from your Elliptical machine, or when getting up from your seat on the airplane to stretch your legs. In those few brief moments, someone could easily steal your book. Not that it is a huge loss monetarily, but it may be tough to replace. Bookstores could very easily be waiting for a new shipment, and time is of the essence in this novel, new game of love. Say you board a flight filled with dreamy, single Stews and you chose a seat next to a guy reading this exact book. Imagine having to sit by and watch another man make a love connection…right before your very eyes. Even worse, if he's the cheap thief that stole your book! (Remember the part about putting your brand on it?)

It's a known fact; men like taking things that belong to other men: things like girls and balls. Stealing a basketball or football is somehow rewarding enough to base a sport around, and it seems especially exciting when the steal is most unforeseen. Think about it. Whether in business, sports, or love, men thrive on the element of surprise, and they love to win at all costs. Being sneaky and sly are both real adrenaline rushes, and something as simple as stealing a book like this could catch on, so don't let it happen to you. Those cheap guys may be the same cheap guys that will one day attempt to steal your honey. So, stay alert and keep your eye on the book at all times. Trust no one.

This guide is not a side of fries to be shared with your buddies. I don't recommend sharing with friends, and I don't recommend letting anyone peek over your shoulder to read it. It just isn't that kind of book. It's not a girlie magazine with airbrushed photos; this is the real deal. If you want to be a major contender and the first to get to "The Fly Girl Market," keep this book out of your friends' sweaty little palms. Friends are friends, but keep in mind that they are indeed your competition. Keep them in the dark as long as possible. Maybe once you have lassoed your own little Fly Filly and you're deciding who'll be standing up for you on your wedding day, you can give them each their own copy as a thank-you gift. But until that day, I highly recommend not sharing; it could easily ruin a friendship.

4. **Hide this book in a safe place.**

Some books are kept in your library or on your coffee table for display. Not this one. This one makes for great kindling, which secret will be revealed in the next chapter. It's not for the recycling bin, nor is it to hand down to a friend. That is the last thing you'll want to do. Competition over a saucy Stew can ruin even a brotherhood friendship. I know I am repeating myself, but it is for your own good. When you've finished this book, hide it. Hide it where your friends won't find it. Being first to the market is key. Don't let your conscience get to you, and don't feel bad for not sharing with friends. First things first. Once you land your own Fly Girl, that's the time to introduce your buddies to her Fly Girl friends. Stewardesses are like a sorority. This close-knit group has a surplus of single Stew friends who are also looking for great datable guys. Take care of your own personal needs first; the rest will follow.

Once you've landed your own steady Stew, it should be safe to share a secret or two with brothers or close friends. Or, if you feel more comfortable working in a pack, go ahead and have all your friends buy a book and make it a group activity where you have your own weekly meetings. Sometimes there is power in numbers. If you prefer to hunt alone, I suggest you be fairly secure in your relationship before introducing her to your pals, and well into the book before taking a chance on losing your girl to an overachiever friend who might feel free flights trump a friendship. Free stuff makes people do bizarre things. I'm not trying to say that your friends would do you that way, but it wouldn't be the first time. Daytime television is filled with stories of friends stealing their best friends' girlfriends, seven days a week.

So, whenever you deem the time is right, go ahead and tell them about this book, but again, be sure to make them buy their own, and make doubly sure they get their own girl. Believe me; once they get a taste of how great it is to date a Stew, they'll do anything and everything in their power to steal her from you. (It saves them from having to buy a ticket.) So read and re-read. Keep it fresh if you want to stay on top. If you are one of the lucky ones who manage to catch and keep the ever-so-busy, never-at-home girl on the fly, you'll need a quick reference every now and then.

5. **Light it up!**

I doubt there are any authors who ask their readers to use their book as kindling once they've finished; maybe I'll be the first. (This is one reason a paperback version is good to buy or at least to have on hand, just for the right moment.) Let me help you set the scene. Imagine holding hands with your sexy Stew on a white sandy beach in front of a crackling, romantic bonfire, while waiting for the sun to set, or perhaps the two of you are snuggled up in a mountain lodge in front of a cozy, stone fireplace watching the snowflakes fall as they blanket the ground. What-ever scenario you prefer, set the perfect scene to enlighten her as to what you've been planning. Be sure to pack the book with you. Remember? By this time, it should show some wear and tear and may even have some highlighted parts you'd like to share. I guar-antee she'll get a thrill when she finds out what you've been up to, and she'll more than likely return a thrill or two as well. Then, twist it; tear it up; light this book on fire! Let it burn it and watch the sparks fly! It'll make for great conversation as you tear out page after page over a wonderful bottle—or two—of her favorite wine. I'm certain she'll appreciate knowing that you took the time and consideration to learn about her life and special needs. If for some odd reason the evening doesn't work out as well as you had hoped, well, you can always buy another book—or steal a friend's.

On-Board Etiquette

Knowing proper airline etiquette is very important if you want to catch the eye of a girl on the fly. Once you have made your reservation on the Love Jet and you are ready to board, follow these simple steps to impress and give yourself a wing up and above all the other guys in line.

Dress Appropriately

No shoes, no shirt, no sex, no kidding. If you want to make a first good impression, make sure you wear appropriate travel attire. Whether you've spent the day at the beach or you're commuting for work, be a clean machine; smell good, or don't smell at all. If you wear cologne, keep it to a minimum.

Come Bearing Gifts

If you want a guaranteed home-run smash hit with any crew member, might I recommend bringing treats on-board? Whether it's a package of M & M's, jellybeans, or trail mix, bring an offering, something sweet (and unopened) that can be shared with the whole crew. (Or not.) You can always keep it for yourself or the return flight if no crew member tickles your fancy. Then again, even if there isn't a single sweetie pie working the flight, look on the bright side; one of the crew members might have a friend or daughter she would like to introduce you to—if you play your sweets right. If the flight is full, there may not be time to strike up a conversation; never give up hope. Keep a positive outlook, make your own opportunities, and keep the candy coming. (Drop the book or candy in the aisle as a crew member walks by, if you must.)

Best Seats in the House

Year after year, I have watched you men rush on-board and hog the aisle seats. It wasn't long after I started working on an airplane that I fully understood the "Passion of the Aisle," especially the ones w'ay in the back. (Just so you know, many airline employees refer to the back end of the aircraft as "the rear." I have always thought it a bit odd to use that terminology, but it is a man's world, after all!) These few, highly-sought-after seats in the rear are like box seats at a baseball game or horse track, or like sitting on the 50-yard line at a football or soccer game. They're a great place to view the lineup. When you're on an airplane, these rare-rear seats are "the seats with a view," or, shall I say, "the view of the seats"?

The lucky boys who get these prime seats can easily lean over into the center of the aisle, peek around their newspaper, and innocently enough check out the "junk in her trunk" (AKA, her backside) as she maneuvers over big feet, broad shoulders, and misplaced bags in order to get wherever she's going. Every voyeur—I mean, man—knows that if she does end up flying over an object left out in the aisle, she'll be searching for a soft lap to land in—preferably the lap of an attentive man. Logic will tell you that this attentive man will be sitting in an aisle seat. Get it?

Just make sure she's not tripping over *your* bag, because that, my friend, would be called an intentional foul on this field of love, and it's absolutely not allowed in your game plan. If you are lucky enough to sit there, it is imperative to be courteous and keep your shoulders, arms, legs, and bags out of the center aisle. The passengers paid for the seat, not the center aisle. The aisle belongs to the crew.

Believe it or not, these prime seats are hot-hot-hot for other reasons, too. Read on.

Eavesdropping

The view is not the only great reason to sit in the rear aisle seats; you're also within listening range to overhear the back galley smack. The whispering and all the juicy stuff the passengers aren't supposed to hear. Personal stuff. Secrets. Smut stuff. Bitching about passengers and Pilots' stuff. Stuff about the good and bad of past and present relationships, along with loads of other naughty stuff men love to overhear. You may also find out things such as what city she lives in; where she goes for happy hour(s); who colors her hair; and whether she has kids, cats, or dogs. You may find out what gym she belongs to, what good swear words she knows or even where she gets "Miss Kitty" tuned up. I know from experience; the back galley is where the smack is at!

Seriously, guys, your choice of seating is crucial. Bypass the over-wing row with extra legroom. If you want to play in the Big Leagues and catch all the action at no additional cost, there is only one place to be: the aisle seats in the rear. They're limited, they're well worth the leg cramps, and they fill up fast. Be sure to get to the airport early; camp out if you have to, and read a good book. And by that, of course, I mean, read this book.

You may have noticed that the men who position, posture, and pay additional fees are always those that board first. These guys are not rookies. They probably bought all the books at the airport bookstore just so no one else could be privy to the secrets that lie within. These are smart guys; they plan ahead. They know that a little extra time or money is well worth getting the best seat in the house. (I say that literally and figuratively, as well.) They are probably carrying this little piece of gold in their briefcase or coat pocket, or maybe they have downloaded it onto their e-book. The true professionals do both; they play every angle. It's hard to be certain, but more than likely you are not alone in your secret quest. Don't think for one moment that you are the only player in the lineup; the well-dressed tie-guy sitting across from you could very easily be using that *Fortune* magazine as a slipcover for this very same book.

If for some reason you don't make it to the first-string seats, do your best to at least get an aisle seat. Just because an opponent beat you to the front line doesn't mean you're not a contender. I know from experience that the underdog sometimes wins the girl in the end. Real winners never give up hope, but if you are going to be a serious player, know the importance of the back-aisle seats.

Prince Charming

You have already passed the first stage with flying colors since you've read this far, so let's continue on a path to success. When the Stewardess comes by to take your beverage order, this is the perfect opportunity to make a subtle move. Pay attention and don't act coy as if you don't see her standing three inches from you. Look directly into her eyes and tell her what you would like to drink. (Make sure it's on the menu.) Don't get needy and start asking for two limes in your drink or only one ice cube. This is your first opportunity to start a light conversation and prove yourself easy. (You know what I mean.)

When the time is right, say something about this book (which you are most certainly reading, if you are paying attention). Keep it simple. Say something like, "I just picked up this book about dating Stewardesses, and it is one of the funniest, enlightening books I have ever read! Have you read it?" Whatever your opening line, be sure to ask a question so it will engage a response and interaction. This way, you're showing her that you're interested in what she thinks. Get it? Turn on the charm. If she has any level of interest, whether for herself personally or a friend or fellow crew member, she'll make the next move. The ball is now in her court. She'll either strike up a clever one-on-one conversation or excuse herself for a moment and return with one or all of the Stews for a group chat. You can't beat that. Believe it or not, as outgoing as Stewardesses may seem, most are too shy to approach a man they are attracted to, especially while most of the passengers are watching their every move. But this type of exchange is good clean fun. If nothing else, you'll be the envy of every man on-board, and you may even get a complimentary cocktail or two—with double limes.

Bag and Body Language

The way a man handles his own bag is important. The way he puts his carry-on into the overhead bin or under the seat in front of him directly reflects his personality and mood. A guy who "shoves, crams, and jams" comes off as a real jerk. A guy who is "smooth, strong, and confident" comes off as ... "smooth, strong, and confident," a real gentleman. If your luggage is too large to fit under the seat in front of you, simply place it into the overhead bin, and without using brute force make sure the compartment door closes. Then, simply re-open the compartment to make it easy for others to identify which bins are available.

If you have a bag or case that fits under the seat in front of you, make sure the strap isn't hanging out into the aisle. You may even earn extra points if you are seen assisting a helpless passenger stow her bag. Keep this in mind: If you have a choice to assist an elderly woman or a young, long-legged blonde, a word to the wise. Pick the gray over the blonde. It's the winning ticket every time.

Posture

Sit up straight, and don't slouch or leave any body parts hanging out in the aisle. You paid for the space from one armrest to the other. If you are a big, broad-shouldered guy, just be conscious and make an attempt to lean out of the aisle as she walks past. Maybe say something to her like, "I know I'm taking up part of your lane. If I don't see you coming, just honk and I'll be happy to move over." As long as she knows you are trying to be considerate, a bump now and then just might be worth the bruise—if the bump involves the right girl.

Manners

Reminder: Be sure to say, "Hello," "Goodbye," "Please," and "Thank you." Show common courtesy. Make your mother proud. This may be that special someone you take home to meet her someday.

Pay attention and be prepared when the in-flight service begins. If you're ordering coffee and would like cream or sugar, be sure to include that in your order so she doesn't have to make an additional round trip. (There may be a fee.)

To Tip or Not to Tip

If you are a shy guy and need a little something to lower your inhibitions, go ahead and order an adult beverage. FYI: For those of you new to drinking and flying, alcohol consumed on an airplane can get you twice as looped as a cocktail on the ground. The altitude will affect the alcohol absorption into your bloodstream, so if it's a long flight, be sure to drink plenty of water, pace yourself, and don't get sloshed. P.S. Have your credit card or drink coupon out and available when you order your adult beverage.

If you would like to offer a tip, do not—I repeat, do not—stuff it in her pocket. (It's probably filled with pretzels and nuts, but if you feel you must, please be discreet and give no less than a $20.) She didn't deliver a lap dance, and with that type of behavior, more than likely there won't be one in your future.

Eye Contact

Have good eye contact with your Stewardess. When she stops to talk to you, look up, acknowledge her, and smile. When the conversation is over, no matter how short or long, when she stops looking at you, that's your signal to go back to whatever you were doing. There is no need to leer.

Also be aware that you may have an audience of eyes watching, other than those of envious male passengers. Stews love to stand in the back galley and study male passengers as they tilt into the aisle like dominos to admire the backsides of females as they walk past. It's much like a choreographed water ballet, only it's with men on an airplane. The heads go in ... the heads go out— like clockwork. It's only natural and quite interesting to watch. A quick peek is acceptable, but just be sure to look into her eyes when you're not on booty watch.

Be Considerate

One thing you can do to get on the good side of a Stew is to have your tray table down and prepared when she arrives with your beverage. More than likely, she will be using only one hand to offer you your beverage, and a napkin may be a part of the hand-off. Do yourself a favor and do not—I repeat, do not—take the napkin without taking the cup, unless you know the magic trick of how to pull a table cloth out from under the table setting without moving any of the crystal or good china!

Two helpful things you can do before leaving the aircraft are cross your seatbelt, and put your armrest down. If you don't, it's like leaving the toilet lid up when you've finished using someone else's restroom. Crews attempt to "tidy up" the cabin as quickly as they can for the new group of boarding passengers, and it's often done in a flurry. If you have time while standing and waiting for everyone to deplane, please do your Stew these two little courtesies. Cabin crews spend hours a day squeezing in between rows of seats to pick up trash off the floor, pull down armrests, pull up tangled seatbelts, and dig deep into seatback pockets. Be a trend-setter. Who knows? If you're lucky enough to land a Stew, you'll be doing both her and yourself a favor, because she'll be coming home with fewer aches and pains, which leads to a much better homecoming... for all.

Be Funny

Try to bring a little humor into her day. If you have a funny joke or two, go ahead and tell her, but keep it clean ... for now.

Don't Be a Dirty Boy

Make sure you leave your area neat and clean. Many people think the crew is paid to pick up the trash and clean the aircraft when passengers leave. This is a false assumption. All ground time, boarding, deplaning, restocking, and cleaning the aircraft are duties performed out of the goodness of their hearts. Maybe people think the crews are compensated because they don't hear the grumbling. Back in the day, the dirty bird had wonderful cleaning fairies that magically appeared at certain cities during ground stop, to vacuum the floors and do a thorough cleaning. Then one day, they magically disappeared, and a box of powdered latex gloves was left in their place. Let's just leave it at that.

Keep in mind the airplane is not a dumping ground, although it may look like one at times. It is in fact the crew's home away from home. You wouldn't toss a banana peel or leave a dirty diaper on your living room carpet, would you? So, please have a heart and do your part to keep your area as clean as you found it, if not cleaner.

Communication Is Key

If your flight was enjoyable, please thank the crew before you leave. If you are making an important phone call as you deplane or don't have an opportunity to verbally acknowledge your crew, at least attempt a simple nod ... something ... anything. Maybe you didn't make a love connection on this particular flight, but you might see Susie Stew out one night "whining" with a group of her cutie pie friends, and if she remembers you as being a charming, well-mannered kind of guy, she may just ask you to join them for a glass of wine or two.

Offer Assistance

Offer to help clean up after the flight. Now, don't freak out over this one. Your gracious offer will never be accepted; it's simply a nice gesture. Your crew will get a giggle out of it, and it's a great way to earn brownie points.

On-Board Taboos

1. Don't stare at her boobs. Large or small.

2. Again, don't stare at her boobs. OK, I have brothers. I know that it's nearly impossible for men not to stare at boobies. Most grew up attached to them in one way or another, so I understand how it might bring back fond memories. Do me a favor: Just try not to stare at them when she is talking to you. There will be other opportunities if you play your cards right. Be patient; show a little public control.

3. If you're flying on a low-class (I mean, low-cost) carrier, don't make a comment regarding the airline being "a cattle car" to a crew member, or to another passenger for that matter. She won't be able to say it out loud, but she will be thinking, "Well then, "Moo-ve!" You will receive zero points for making that comment, and if you think about it, it makes you sound like an animal … full of bull.

4. Low-cost carriers do not have a First Class section, so don't be a smart ass and embarrass yourself by asking the worn-out question "Where's First Class?" Again, she'll bite her lip to be polite and will give you a forced smile, but she'll definitely be thinking, "It's obviously No Class, pal. Welcome, I'm bored!"

5. Do not mimic the Stewardess as she is doing her emergency demonstrations. Remember way back into your early childhood, when someone would mimic you. Remember how irritating it was? Remember telling them,

"Stop mimicking me"? Remember when they didn't stop and you gave them the ol' knuckle sandwich or hit them over and over in the same spot on the fatty part of their shoulder? Need I go on?

6.   Don't shake your cup at her if you need another beverage. She might think you have a nervous disorder.

7.   Don't mumble under your breath to the guy sitting next to you, "Boy, I'd like a swing like that in my backyard" as she walks away. Another Stew may be standing behind your row listening.

8.   Don't ask her if she has any dental floss; that's just weird.

9.   When she asks, "What would you like to drink?" don't respond, "Steak and eggs over easy." For those of you who haven't really thought this line through, you can't drink steak and eggs. Your response is contrived, and it shows that you have poor listening skills. Guys, heads up: It's a lame line that is used over and over. Those of you who use this line know who you are. Please, add this to your own "things to do" list: Get some new material. Stews really do have a good sense of humor and would absolutely love to hear a new line or two. The non-hilarious "steak and eggs" line may have been funny the first time, 20 plus years ago, but it's not so funny now. By the way, you'll know if your low-cost carrier Stewardess is "seasoned" if she responds, "Steak and eggs? Yes, sir, right after the movie!" (For those of you who have never had the wonderful experience of flying a low-cost carrier, most do not have assigned seating, nor do they show movies onboard.)

10.   Don't tell her she looks tired. Believe me, she knows how she looks, and what's more important to remember is— guess what?—she is tired of hearing it. She knows. She knows. She looks tired.

11.   Don't blame or reprimand a Stewardess for something she was not responsible for. For example, "she" did not lose

your bag. (She probably never touched your bag, and, for that matter, if you took an attitude with the person at the counter who checked your bag, that's probably why it was re-routed through Buffalo on its way from Las Vegas to Los Angeles.) In addition, "she" did not make you miss your connection the last time you flew and your flight was late. She has absolutely nothing to do with the arrival or departure time of an airplane.

12. Don't ask a Stewardess who is wearing her smile upside down why the other perky, young Stewardess with the Kool-Aid mustache and sappy smile has so much energy. There is a real simple answer: The one with the mustache is brand new; the other, used. Period.

13. Don't hit the emergency call button just because you need another pack of nuts or a cherry for your rum and Coke (unless you are seriously cute and available). The emergency call button's primary use is to alert crew members of an emergency on-board, such as a fire or heart attack. Years ago, if an emergency call button was illuminated, all cabin crew members would drop whatever they were doing and dash to save the day. Nowadays, the emergency call button is recyclable. It is used and reused, and used again, day in and day out, for things like an emergency soda or another round for the boys, making it difficult for the crew to know which call button to address first when more than one illuminates at a time. How are they to distinguish between the passenger having a serious heart attack and the one having a heart attack because he wants another cocktail? Do the math. Please press the call button only if there is a life-threatening emergency. Plus, FYI: For any of you who happen to be germ phobic, I have never seen a call button being cleaned—ever.

14. Don't walk to the galley and immediately ask her if the lavatory is empty. Believe it or not, Stews are not on permanent Potty Patrol. Be a responsible adult and prove you know how to read; at least attempt to locate the indicator

that states whether it is occupied or vacant. Many times, the lavatory sign is in two languages. "Ocupadu" is, of course, Spanish for "Occupied." A green signal on the door means it is vacant. Red, of course, means occupied. Still, it is possible to be fooled; airplane doors aren't the most expensive ever made, and sometimes the latches may have slipped, relaying incorrect information. If you are standing around waiting for an extended period of time for the restroom to become vacant, don't just stand there; say something nice about her hair or her shoes. Just say something nice about anything, and watch how easy it is to strike up a conversation. Offer her gum or a mint if you have some; it's a nice way to break the ice. Stews are rarely offered anything, than trash. Be a trendsetter. Offer goodies.

15. Learn what the word "vacant" means. Simple: It means empty. While we are on the subject, a green sign means "Go. The lavatory is empty." No one would believe how many times a Stewardess must tell a passenger what vacant means and what a green dot means. Now, everyone should know. Pass it on.

16. Don't pull on the ashtray embedded in the lavatory door, thinking that doing so will open the door; it will not. The ashtray will, however, make an awful clanging noise as it hits the floor, causing everyone around to look at you and take notice of your embarrassment.

17. A word to the wise: Never let anyone see you take a newspaper, magazine, or reading material into the lavatory. (It makes people wonder just how long you might be planning on staying in the "lav" … and why.) Then again, this book should never be left out in the open, unattended. Put it in your pocket and take it with you. If you end up waiting in line, bring the book out and start up a conversation. Make good use of your time. Talking about the book to fellow passengers and crew members makes for good conversation and will certainly make your waiting time go

faster. When it's your turn to use the "lav," be sure to put the book back in your pocket before entering. (P. S. Do I need to tell you that girlie magazines on the airplane are an absolute no-no?)

18. If at all possible, try to take care of "serious biz-ness" at home or at least in the airport before you board. This is an area where you really need to plan ahead. Don't eat your bran muffin while waiting to board a six-hour flight. Try to flush your body of toxic waste the night before. Herbal teas or coffee, a cigarette—whatever it takes to make you go boom-boom ... at home. It is a real turn-off when a man stays in the lavatory for a "questionable length of time," only to exit and be faced with a line of onlookers questioning whether they dare enter as the vicious, toxic fumes linger after him. Being a Pepé Le Pew is a definite turn-off, and by the way, you don't stand a chance in @#*% if you accidentally leave a "roadie" in the bowl. Double check – Double flush, if you must.

19. Do not poke your Fly Girl. Although some may have a little extra padding these days, they are still not human pincushions. Poking is not acceptable. It was not acceptable to poke schoolgirls, and it is not acceptable to poke Fly Girls. If you need a good poke, boys, well, check the Yellow Pages. Seriously, you'll find pages and pages listed under "Escort."

20. Don't leave your fly open. Sunshine will not make "Mr. Wiggles" grow.

21. Do not ask her for a bite of her sandwich or ask her if she brought one for you. Would you like some stranger to walk over to your lunch table and ask you for a bite?

22. Don't ignore her when she asks you to turn off your cell phone or electronic device. You should have turned it off by the time the aircraft doors close and before the emergency demonstrations begin. When an announcement is made to turn off any and all electronic devices or anything with an on and off switch, please do it—the first time.

Don't make a Stew do her rendition of your kindergarten teacher, who stood over you making sure you put your toys away and listened during class. If for some reason you feel you must linger on the phone and a Stew has to ask you individually to turn it off, say something like, "Oh, I was just saying goodbye to my mother." And don't forget to apologize.

23. Don't ask how you can become a Stewardess. If you are interested in getting to first base, keep the conversation based around her personally. (But for those who really would like to know, here is your answer: You apply on line, and just like the thousands of other applicants, you wait for a letter.)

24. Don't pull a "Helen Keller" when she comes to take your drink order or hand you a snack. A "Helen Keller" is when a passenger doesn't bother to make eye contact but simply "swats" and dismisses her like a pesky fly. I don't read sign, so I can only assume "the swat" is their very own personal sign for "I AM AN IDIOT and it's best you move on, or I might rub off on you." I am quite certain a school would not teach such behavior. Suggestion: Lose the swat sign.

25. Oh, by the way, did I mention, "Don't stare at her boobs"?

26. Last, but not least, never ever—ever!—tell her to "SMILE." Believe me, if she thought you were handsome and she was interested, she would already be smiling, from ear to ear.

Here's Your Sign

In every sport and aspect of life, timing is crucial. The second the Pilot turns off the "Fasten Seatbelt" sign, the gates to the paddocks open, and the race is on. If there are single fillies on-board, more than likely you will need to jockey for position. Keep one hand on the buckle and ready to snap. You may hear a succession of snapping-turtle sounds, as your competition's seatbelt buckles are released.

While you're confined to your seat and waiting for the bell to ring, take time to scout your surroundings. This is when you'll realize your choice of seating is crucial. Also understand that your flirting time may be limited, because the "Fasten Seatbelt" sign goes on and off as the Pilot deems necessary. (Pilots who date Stews have been known to keep the seatbelt sign illuminated throughout the whole flight if they think a good-looking stud might be on-board. Then again, whether or not one of the Stews is a sweetheart, they may just deem the crew to be part of their herd. You can't be certain of how the male mind will work.) No matter what, be prepared for the ringing of the bell.

Here is a list of prerequisites to a smooth approach:

1. Be sure to unbuckle your seatbelt before you try to get up. This is a definite prerequisite to standing. Remember there is a luggage bin overhead. The second or two it takes to bang your head may cause you to be second in line—plus, you don't want to start out feeling stupid.

2. If you have a mint, pop it. Save an extra for her ... just in case.

3. Make sure the crew is finished with their service before you walk to the back galley. It is very difficult for the girls to keep track of what drinks to pour, so don't attempt to talk to them during their service. Wait around for a little while if you have been premature with your approach. Timing is everything.

4. A word to the wise: For those of you who already wear a wedding ring and have plans to take it off just to partake in this new, exciting on-board game, Don't Do It! Stews can see the mark of a wedding band from half a plane away. So, don't try the quick slip. Leave that sly feat to the Pilots. (If by some chance you decide to disregard my advice and end up losing your ring on the airplane, check with the Lost and Found. They always have quite an assortment to choose from: gold, silver, and platinum, with or without diamonds.)

5. If you chicken out and/or the Stewardess had to return to the cabin for something, step into the lavatory to regroup. Be sure to read the sign on the door to ensure it is vacant before turning the handle.

6. After entering, make sure you close the door tight and lock it. Too many times, the door is ajar when you think it's locked. You don't want to get caught with your pants down. Not in there.

7. Look in the mirror to make sure you don't have any food stuck between your teeth or a long nose hair hanging out for all to see. If you do, find some way to deal with it. While you are in there, check for "bats in the cave." (This is a nice little way to say, "Check your nose for ... stuff.")

8. Wear shoes when entering the lavatory. The liquid on the floor is not water, nor residue from Mr. Clean. Yellow, yes. Mr. Clean, no.

9.   Always double check to make sure you flushed.

10. Before you leave, double check to ensure no tissue is stuck to the bottom of your shoe or hanging out the back of your pants.

11. If you have a toothbrush with you, use it. Discreetly let the Stewardess see it in your hand. It takes away from the real reason you are "going" in there and lets her know you take good care of yourself.

12. If at all possible, use the lavatory in the front of the airplane if you have to do more than tinkle. If you have a light cologne, attempt to "cover your trail," so to speak. But seriously, if at all possible, try to take care of serious business before you step onto the aircraft.

Remember, "Due to heightened security standards, we can no longer have anyone standing, waiting, or lining up to use the forward restroom," so if you are going to loiter, boys, you are welcome to loiter in back. If you are lucky enough to have had some good eye contact for even a brief moment as she flew past, get up out of your seat and saunter on over to the back galley. If she's stationed up front and is remotely interested, she'll find the time to walk to the back of the aircraft. Whether she's working up front, in the middle, or in the back, if she's single and scouting, you'll find her in the rear of the aircraft. It's a simple fact.

For those of you in disbelief, go ahead and try to flirt up front. If you are lucky, you may get a flash flirt, but the flirt with substance and the possibility of a real phone number exchange will most likely happen in the back of the aircraft. Beyond airline security restrictions, up-front flirting just looks bad to the rest of the *Lookie Lous. Lookie Lous* are the married men nervously sitting on the sidelines, twisting their golden band back and forth, their minds planning all sorts of scenarios they would be using if they were still players.

For the serious contenders, there are a couple of things to consider when flirting with a Fly Girl. She may look cool, calm, and collected on the outside, but she is first and foremost a professional and is on high alert at all times, ready to block any terrorist act at any given moment. Keep in mind, if you look suspicious in any way, she might be envisioning giving you the ol' Hi-Karate move as you attempt to hand her your business card. So take that into consideration, and make sure you don't say anything inappropriate or act in any disrespectful way. Be a gentleman at all times. Save the bad boy behavior for later.

Another thing to consider is whether or not you'll need to fake a charley horse. If the bell goes off and you aren't quite as fast as the guy in front of you, don't be afraid to put up a man-block. All's fair in love and war. Sticking out your foot with the intention of tripping up your competition is fair game. It's all in the presentation. It's got to look real, at least to the rest of the crowd. You won't want to get an intentional foul flag from the sideline referees. Another play that works in a clutch is to ring your emergency call button and fake a faint. This is where the player (you) fakes like he is passed out and in need of immediate resuscitation. It's a real attention getter. A little open mouth-to-mouth never hurt a guy. There are no boundaries here, boys. If you are lucky, she'll come running, forgo the plastic mask, and go right for the full-on lip-to-lip lock!

What a great way to find out if your lips are perfectly matched and to see if she's interested and naughty enough to take a chance on a good ol' fashioned spit swap. If it feels like a good match, go ahead and play dead for a while, but don't play "full-on dead," as there will be another Stew just seconds away, arriving with the AED kit to shock you to your senses. When you find your shirt suddenly being ripped off your body, that is your indication to take a deep breath and open your eyes. Finding your bare back on a dirty carpet is the red flag to make a miraculous recovery. I repeat, "Make a miraculous recovery!" Because the next step after having your shirt ripped off is having your chest shaved … with a dull razor. Having Super Stew shave your chest in public might be a turn-on, but the next step is electrifying! This is where I recommend drawing the line. Take my advice and wake up before the game gets to the sticky pads.

If you're not a daredevil and would rather take a safer route, simply saunter to the back of the aircraft when the time is right and start a little chitchat. If another player has arrived before you, don't worry. Take this opportunity to wedge your way in between the two. Don't be rude; tap the guy on his shoulder and say, "Excuse me, my wife and I are trying to decide where to celebrate our second honeymoon," or just join in on the conversation and may the best man win.

If you are on a one-on-one basis, take the next step and ask her the most frequently asked question: "Where are you based?" Although it's a seemingly simple question, the answer can be complex. So, listen carefully. If she says something like, "Houston, but I am kind of ready for a change," the gates are open. That response, my friend, is short for "Keep talking." If her answer is, "Houston; the restroom is open," that is short for "Keep walking." In the latter case, use the restroom, take your pride back to your seat, and buckle in. Sometimes, Stews are just not in the mood for flirting.

Role-Play

Let's role-play. Imagine yourself walking to the back galley. You are now one-on-one with Susie Stew. She hasn't turned to tell you, "The restroom is vacant," nor is she in the middle of her service. Now is the perfect time to strike up a light conversation. The following five questions are great icebreakers and alternatives to the number one most popular question of the year, "Where are you based?"

1. How long have you been working with the airline?
2. What is your favorite vacation spot?
3. Where did you grow up?
4. Have you read *How to Do a Stew*?
5. Do you like coffee, beer, or wine?

If it's a short flight and you're in a crunch for conversation, skip items 1-4 and go directly to item 5. If it is a leisurely flight, go ahead and ask all five, but the last question is always the most remembered. It's kind of like when someone you haven't heard from in a very long time calls you to make small-talk, and at the very end of the conversation, you find out the real reason they called: They have an agenda.

If you have a chance to ask these simple five questions, you'll definitely find out if you have anything in common. That's why the last question is so important: Almost everyone in the airline industry likes some sort of wine or booze—every Stewardess I know, anyway. So, if you think there might be a love connection and you'd like to see her out of uniform, so to speak, wrap up the conversation with something like "Would you like to meet for a cup of coffee or a glass of wine next time you're in town?" That's when you'll find out if she's taken the hook. Stews love their comfort drink, and most are cautious about spending their own coin. Coffee and wine are the top two favorites, so now you've got her attention. "Bingo," she answers. "Yes, that sounds great!" Congratulations! You are another step closer to a lifetime of free space-available flights!

When setting a date, try to choose a day when she's neither going to nor coming in from work. When Stews—even seasoned ones—are preparing to leave town, there is never enough time to get necessary tasks accomplished, and that day can become hectic. On her return, her flight may be running late or circling due to weather, and she may not have an opportunity to call ahead of time. In travel, there are too many variables out of her control, so until a man gets used to the "ups and downs" of the industry, I suggest planning dates on her days off, or be prepared to drink alone.

A beverage date is the perfect first date. It is inexpensive and quick. When you meet, keep the conversation short and sweet. Let her know you appreciate her taking time to meet with you, but also be subtle, letting her know you too are carving out time from your schedule to get to know her. Stewardesses have been trained to be punctual to a fault, but sometimes they over-book personal appointments and may have to cancel at the last moment. Don't be the booking that gets cancelled. Make sure you let her know you are making her a priority; otherwise, you may have to take a delay or rebook. Time flies in the life of a Stewardess, and it may be weeks until she's available again.

When you first call to ask her out, you may have to leave a message. Understand that she might be out of range for hours or may not be able to contact you until the next day or so. One thing you will learn early on is that a Stewardess will call you back when she is good and ready. Part of her job as a Stewardess is to be an infinite source of information day in and day out, and sometimes she just doesn't feel like talking. Stewardesses are bombarded with idle conversation from the time they step onto the airport van to the time they are dropped off in the parking lot. People love to ask the girls in uniform questions.

When she does return your phone call, be sure not to start grilling her with questions about her flight, or medical and dental benefits. You'll find out this information all in good time. Keep the conversation simple; food, wine, animals, family, and friends are the usual first-date topics.

If you fall into the category of a "GUM," the game is quite different. A "geographically undesirable man" lives in a different city, state, or sometimes a mere zip code, and has additional challenges. A relationship with a GUM is very time consuming and normally short lived. For those who make it to the sleepover stage, the sex may be hot for the first few overnights but as the relationship develops, be prepared to snuggle up to snoring once the newness wears off.

Airline travel is taxing enough if you are a vacationer or business traveler—even more so if you travel for a profession. Crossing different time zones and jumping onto another flight as soon as she gets off work is not on a Fly Girl's dating wish list. Imagine going right back to the office on your days off, not having enough time to go home to shower and change to visit your new love. The last thing a Stew wants to do after a long day on the dirty bird is pack yet again for another overnight, especially if it's unpaid. True, Stews have free travel benefits, but they are not positive-space seats; they are known as "non-revenue" or "space-available" seats. Tracking the next open flight to her man friend's destination can easily mean several additional hours in airports as well as the possibility of being taken off the flight unexpectedly if she has several stops and/or plane changes. There is no guarantee she will even board the flight. If the flight is full, there may be a chance she can ride the "jump seat," the hard, little pull-down covered bench in the back of the aircraft that is available only to airline personnel. Many times, employees won't get approval to board until the very last minute, so she will always be checking for the next available flights and calling you frequently with updates and possibilities.

Flying "non-rev" is great as long as the flights are wide open; if not, she may have to abort all efforts and try her luck the next day, or week for that matter. Many times, it's just better for all concerned to pay for a ticket so she knows she will arrive on time with a smile on her face and can return home without any question.

When she finally arrives at her new love's destination and falls into his arms, no doubt she will be weary and wondering what the sleeping arrangements are. She'll be tattered around the edges and sporting dark circles under her eyes, but one sure thing will ease the anxiety: wine. Any adult beverage will do for a weary Stew, but I recommend learning her preference ahead of time and having the cabinet stocked accordingly. The truth about booze and travel is twofold. At first, it is the fuel to the fire, but as familiarity grows, a good bottle of wine suddenly turns from aphrodisiac into deep snooze enhancer. Get ready; it's a Flight Attendant fact.

After the love fest is over, you'll be driving your sweet Stew back to the airport, ready for departure rain or shine. Remember, she'll be traveling space available again. She'll need to get through airport security lines and find her gate, hoping there is an available seat. So be sure to arrive at least an hour or two early. Beyond that, if you haven't spent a lot of time traveling, you'll soon find out about all the possible complications, such as weather delays, cancellations due to mechanicals, and all sorts of other unexpected surprises.

You may end up having a visitor—good or bad—for another day or two, or you might spend a few extra hours in the airport; they're all just part of the wonderful world of non-rev travel. Flying free may have a nice ring to many, but it also comes with several strings attached. When she finally does return home, there is barely enough time to pay some past-due bills, kiss the dog, and pick up a pressed uni-tard at the corner cleaners. Trying to squeeze a love life between work and sleep can be difficult, to say the least, and traveling on her days off can be about as much fun as food poisoning, especially when traveling space available.

Story Time: Cactus League

I have been urged to share a few stories throughout this book, though I hesitate, because my stories are everyday good-girl stories. I don't have any smut stories to tell, and even if I did, that's not what this book is about. Each story that was shared with me was told in strict confidence, and I owe it to my sister Stews and to myself to uphold our code of ethics. United We Stand, Divided We Fall. Hang Together, or Hang Separately. Many of us have grown up together. Over the years, we've developed friendships and bonds that will last a lifetime. We don't have to attend reunions to rekindle old friendships as we do when we want to see our high school or college chums; through the years, it seems we all somehow find a way to keep tabs on one another. If we don't fly with a particular friend, we fly with someone who knows someone who knows someone. Sooner or later, most of us cross paths in an airport security line, going from gate to gate between flights, or we catch a few accidental moments while standing in line for coffee or a sandwich on the go. Most of my friends were single and we were in our 20s when we were hired. The hiring profile was more monochromatic; today, a more colorful syndicate flies the skies. We have stood by one another through marriages, divorces, and raising children; through blue skies and troubled waters.

If you are looking for a book about how to meet a "Slutty Stew," this book will help you find her; it will also help you find a "Susie Stew". Thousands are out there flying the skies and buzzing around town; they come in all shapes and sizes, and they all pack their own personalities. If you *just* want stories about hot

Stews and details of joining the mile-high club over the Swiss Alps and such, blogs and books aplenty have already been written. Then again, you can always Google it!

The story you are about to read is my first geographically undesirable dating story.

It was early March, and the Cactus League spring training was in the air. I was working in the back of the aircraft from Phoenix (my home base) to San Francisco and minding my own business when a very tan, friendly man appeared and started up a conversation. Steven was a smooth-talker. He reminded me of the Fuller Brush salesman who used to go door to door selling vacuums and household stuff when I was a kid. The kind of guy a girl's dog would let into the house and then get his ball to play catch with, whether she was home or not.

Steven and his best friend, Max, were returning home after a week spent in Santa Fe, followed by another sun-'n-fun bake-off in Phoenix for baseball's spring training. Within a few minutes, his friend joined us; the two of them were adorable. We all talked without anyone soliciting anyone; it was as if I were talking to my brothers. No one was putting on any moves, and there were no sexual innuendoes. It was just a nice exchange of general information regarding where we all lived, what places we had traveled to, and your everyday subjects between a Stew and passengers. I did notice that Max was wearing a beautiful rose gold watch, circa 1950, on his left wrist, and I couldn't help but ask him about it. Max loved combing swap meets and flea markets across the country, looking for good finds. He most certainly had an eclectic look, with his curly black hair, white tee shirt sleeves rolled up, great old 501 blue jeans, and worn black cowboy boots.

As the airplane began its descent, they returned to their seats, but not before giving me their phone numbers. In parting, Steven said, "Next time you have a stop in San Francisco, give us a call and we'll take the whole crew out on the town." I thought that was a very generous, unassuming offer. I liked their style. I told them that I rarely had layovers in San Francisco, but I would most certainly give them a call if I did. Before they stepped off the airplane, they both turned to wave goodbye.

Oddly enough, within a couple of weeks, I was on reserve and scheduled to overnight in San Francisco; my flight was landing at about 3 p.m. and I'd be leaving the next morning. The crew I was flying with was both tired and married, and going out on the town as a group was not in the cards that evening. When I arrived at the hotel, I called Steven, only because I found his card at the bottom of my bag first. As I was leaving a short message, I dug a bit deeper and found Max's number. When Max answered, I could hear saws and hammering in the background; he apologized for the noise, as he was in the middle of renovating a downtown Berkeley loft he had just purchased. He seemed happy to hear from me and after a short conversation, he offered to pick me up for dinner. I didn't think to ask if Steven was going to join us, but I wouldn't have been surprised if he had. It didn't feel like a one-on-one date; it felt more like a friend taking time to show another friend around town.

It was Chamber of Commerce weather in the city. Max and I walked through North Beach and wandered into a charming restaurant situated across from the Saints Peter and Paul Church, where Joltin' Joe DiMaggio and his second wife, Marilyn Monroe, had their famous wedding photos taken in 1954. It was all very casual but romantic, and as cliché as it may sound, I guess I did leave a little part of my heart in San Francisco that night. It was the first time I had ever gone out on a date on an overnight, and I never intended it to be an actual date. As it turned out, it was the first of many great dates and days to come.

Two years later, if I wasn't working, I was spending the majority of my time in the Bay Area or flying to Los Angeles to meet Max on his business trips. Every month, I rearranged my schedule so we could spend time together, which was time consuming, and frustrating to boot. I never knew for certain if I would be able to get on a flight, and I spent many untold hours in airports waiting for the next available flight. Traveling back and forth, combined with juggling my schedule to meet his while still trying to make a living, was difficult, to say the least. I looked like the dawn of the living dead most of the time, and when Max offered to help out financially I accepted, as it would enable me to give a trip or two away each month and not feel I was burning the candle at both ends. It was generous for him to offer support, and it sounded like a good idea ... at the time.

When this exchange in our relationship happened, the dynamics of our relationship changed as well. Max seemed to get a bit more possessive of my time. After all, he was paying me, right? I knew he meant well and the offer came from his heart, but from that point on, whenever I needed to return to Phoenix to work, he always drove extremely slow, or we left for the airport late ... anything to make my experience going back filled with stress. It didn't take me long to figure out that our financial arrangement wasn't as good as had been originally intended. It certainly wasn't working for me; the airline owned my time once I clocked in, but my free time was my time, and it was not for sale, at any price.

Shortly after I stopped rearranging my life, Max asked me to marry him. I'm not sure why, except perhaps for the fact that we had regressed from spending weeks together to spending a few sporadic days together. When I went back to my usual four-day workweek, it became nearly impossible to schedule our days off together. He had a full life in the Bay Area and a flourishing new business in the music industry. His family and all his friends, with the exception of me, lived in the area. I think he missed his best friend, and that is the main reason he asked me to marry him. His proposal actually came with an ultimatum ... "or else." I will be very honest; if it had not been for the "or else," I may have said, "Yes." I was never good at ultimatums.

Max's friend Steven and I have stayed friends for over 20 years. He is happily married to a gorgeous wife and has four wonderful children. A group of our close friends in the Bay Area formed a partnership and own real estate together. You may have guessed: Steven's forte is real estate. He is a great salesman and an equally a great friend. It has worked out beautifully. Max fell in love and married a local girl, and they are, I hope, living happily ever after.

Just Plane Tired

It was late one night, and I was going on my 11th hour. I looked like someone had beaten me with an ugly stick. ALL day and night. The weather had been horrific throughout the entire trip, and my last flight from Las Vegas to Phoenix was over three hours late. Vegas to Phoenix is my very least favorite flight in the world, especially when it's late. It's always full of losers (read into that whatever you want) too cheap to pay for an extra day at their hotel; they've been wandering in and out of casinos, gambling, drinking, and stinking, without a room in which to shower or shave. Most men have lost their shirts at the tables and are coming home with a little coin and a whole lot of attitude.

When the last flight of the night is uber-late, I'd swear some Pilots try to break the sound barrier. Some may have flights to catch; others, I think, just get a kick out of playing Maverick and Goose. Making a flight in record time can be exciting and fun for the Pilots, but it is a different story for the crews, who are tumbling around in the back galley slinging drinks and preparing for the final flight of the night.

So there I was late at night, spread eagle in the back galley trying to keep from tumbling over, and the lights were on low (for my own personal enhancement). I was trying to take inventory and close out the kitchen while dealing with a Major League migraine. That's when I saw him. Out of the corner of my eye appeared a very attractive man, standing there looking at me. I quickly glanced at the lavatory sign to see if it was available. It was in fact vacant. The "Fasten Seatbelt" sign was illuminated, and I could tell by the way he was standing that he wasn't there to make an office call. He was there to chat ... with me.

He did most of the talking and asked the usual questions. After a few minutes, we discovered that not only did we live in the same city, but we lived within five minutes of one another. He was a "GDM." A "geographically desirable man" was hard to find—especially one that was tall, attractive, fit, and interested in me. Long story short: This handsome, rare-to-find on a "cheap-seat airline" man was a Stew's dream come true. At first I thought he must be a freak or a stalker; I mean, who else would be interested in a girl who looked as whooped as I did?

I remember feeling awkward and thinking, "Self, something must be seriously wrong with this geographically desirable, very handsome man, who, if we began dating, could save me an untold number of dollars in doggie care, even more in parking fees, and who could very well know how to keep my pool water from turning green. But why would a man who appeared to be anything but the usual 'late-night Vegas loser' be standing back here in turbulence talking to me, when I look like someone mopped the restroom floor with my head? What gives? Something must be wrong with him, because I look like I was just tossed out of a tornado. He must be attracted to victims, victims with hair who look like they were just released from a two-week stay in a hospital. Hat hair; that kind of hair." Anyway, it didn't take long for me to eliminate that date and toss him into the "just another nut" file. So, I politely told him, "The restroom is open." That was the end of that love story.

I look back on past opportunities and wonder what would have happened if I hadn't been just so plane tired. Perhaps he could have been the man of my dreams; standing right there in front of me could have been the man who lived just down the street and who could have picked me up and driven me to the airport and taken care of my dogs. Or was he just another regular, down-on-his-luck Bob who was looking to save himself some money and "marry me, fly free"?

The moral of the Stew story is this: Just don't take it personally, guys, if Susie Stew responds, "The restroom is open." Sometimes, she's just had a very long day, and no matter how adorable she might find you, even the slightest attempt for her to make light conversation may just send her into a two-bottle-of-wine night, and that could get expensive. There is no guarantee that you will make a love connection on your first try, so take Dr. Lee's advice: Practice, practice, practice! Another Stew is out there flying about, and maybe she hasn't had a bad hairy day.

Part III

Catch Her on the Fly

Stage I: Woo Your Stew

Catching a girl on the fly is one thing; landing her is another.

It has been rumored that Stews are easy; that's just plane Pilot talk. Believe me, they are anything but. It takes a good man with a good-sized tool box to even begin to "Woo a Stew." Now, we all know that it's not just the size that matters; he has to know how to use his tools as well. If you're that kind of confident man, you have enormous potential in landing a Fly Girl, but on your first date, I highly recommend keeping all conversations light and easy. Be subtle; don't take her home and show her your tools. Keep her guessing, but definitely let her know that you are good with your hands and know how to use them.

On the first date, she may tell you a few stories of her own personal travel experiences from weird to wonderful, some good, some bad, some fun, and some not so fun. Feel free to share your own funny story or great vacation experiences, but do not dwell on negative experiences like weather delays and lost luggage. Steer more towards what your own personal strengths are, such as giving a mean foot rub and loving to work on household repairs.

As in all dating, I recommend staying away from the top two argument-inducing issues: politics and religion. Might I suggest a few safer subjects:

1. Her pets
2. Her family

3. Where she went to high school or college

4. Her favorite vacations, and where she would like to travel

5. Sports she likes to watch or participate in

6. Her favorite restaurants or coffee bars

7. Her favorite bar (which is usually the one closest to her house)

These seven topics should get you through anywhere from 15 minutes to a great afternoon; they might even whisk you right into dinner and a movie, depending on her interest level, as well as yours. Two topics she'll more than likely cover during the first date or two are whether or not she needs a pet sitter and what her hectic work schedule is like. If she does have a pet and you happen to take it upon yourself to take care of her pooch or kitty whenever she is away, you, my friend, are a shoo-in, especially if you were already thinking of offering before you read the last couple of sentences!

Stews love their pets, and they are constantly looking for a good pet sitter. If she feels you're the kind of guy she trusts her home and pets with, that, my friend, is a great sign. You'll more than likely make it to the next stage. P.S. If you are allergic to animals, call your physician for an appointment immediately. Then, make plans for the next date.

Speaking of Dogs...

I have met some very nice men on my flights, and I have dated a few. I dated a male Flight Attendant for a couple of years, a Pilot for a year, and two passengers whose relationships lasted between one and two years. Meeting men on a flight is the easy part; what's rare is following through with more than a few phone calls to see if there is anything other than a good flirt going on. I've watched my girlfriends get all giddy and squirrelly about exchanging phone numbers with men they have met on-board. Sure, there have been a few late-night rendezvous, but few worked out for any length of time, and none that I know of worked out permanently.

The majority of men I've met on the airplane were geographically undesirable, and after a while, returning missed phone messages and talking about how you wish you had time to get together becomes redundant. Constantly planning how to get together, who's going to take care of your dogs or kids—well, it can just plane wear a girl out. In all honesty, you can meet plenty of ready, willing, and available single men through friends or the local hangout, and sometimes it's just easier. I guess it depends on if a girl is looking for a date or a mate. It definitely makes a difference.

Here is a story about just that.

Good-Time Charlie

It was an exceptionally sunny day, and my flight was scheduled to go to Seattle, Washington, and then onto ... somewhere. I was stationed in the back of the airplane (the best place to meet men, as you will recall) when I noticed a very attractive, well-dressed businessman boarding the flight. He was in the first boarding group; he walked to the back of the aircraft and took an aisle seat. (Smart move.) Great haircut. Sport coat: Armani. My kind of guy. I, on the other hand, was sporting an ensemble of wrinkled Docker-type pants that were borderline "waders," marred tennis shoes from kicking in ill-fitting metal containers of beer and wine, and a once-white shirt, now spotted with the fresh remains of an exploded Coke can. My Dalmatian look.

It's rare for me to find a man I am attracted to on any of my flights. It's also equally rare to find Armani, and it's equally embarrassing to stand in front of a very together, nice-looking man when you look like you've just spent the afternoon at a paint ball party. I knew right off the bat that I didn't stand a chance with Mr. Clean, so I decided to make the best of the situation: I drew his attention to someone else. A tactical plan of diversion.

En route to this handsome, clean man, I noticed two chatty women sitting a couple of rows behind him, on the opposite side of the aircraft. After asking them a few questions, I found out they were on vacation and visiting Seattle for the first time. They hadn't a clue where to go or what to do. That gave me an idea. I could play matchmaker and pawn off these two girls, taking the heat off how horrible I looked. It's actually an old tactic my girlfriends and I used in college when we wanted to meet a guy but were afraid of getting shut down ourselves. One of us would approach the "man in question" and tell him that one of our shy girlfriends was interested in him. At that point, he would say he was already in a relationship, not interested, or interested in the one doing the talking. No harm, no foul.

So, I gave it the ol' college try, not thinking for a moment that he would actually notice me. It was purely a way to make it more comfortable for me to even talk to him, considering the "spotted" state I was in. Their clothes were clean; their pants were just the right length; their leather boots were unscuffed. Perfect candidates for Mr. Clean.

I decided to make an announcement to the crowd, stating there were a couple of good-looking single ladies vacationing for a week in Seattle for the first time, and if any single men on-board were interested in chaperoning two single, off-the-charts cute babes, now would be the time to identify themselves. I was surprised that no hands went up; then again, few listen to announcements. "Mr. C" didn't even look up; he seemed more interested in his paperwork than listening to or participating in my on-board dating game, but I hadn't given up. Not yet.

A few minutes later, when we started our in-flight beverage service, instead of asking him what he would like to drink, I asked him straight up, "Are you single and available?" (There wasn't a gold band on his finger.) He looked up and replied, "Yes." So, I quickly explained about the two ladies looking for a guide through the Northwest Passage and handed him their contact number. (I had already pointed out Mr. Businessman to the ladies, to make sure he was a suitable candidate, and their contact number was in my hand and ready to go.) I winked at the girls, continued on, and let the love gods take over from there.

As we began our descent, "Mr. C" came to the back of the aircraft and asked if my crew was going to overnight in Seattle. I told him we were actually working a round trip from Phoenix to Seattle and would be returning to Phoenix that day. That's when he introduced himself and asked me if I had time on the ground for a cup of coffee. I was caught totally off guard, to say the least.

I thought "Charlie" was just making small-talk as he waited for the lavatory to become available. (And, yes, to all of those wondering, I did check to see if it was vacant or not.) It was the first flight of the day, and even though I was stained and wrinkled, my hair did look pretty cute, and I was in just the right frame of mind to say, yes.

The line for coffee was, fortunately, quite long, which gave us just enough time to find out we both loved golf, lakes, and the outdoors and that we actually lived within a 20-mile radius ... over 20 years ago. Our conversation was short but sweet; we exchanged phone numbers, and I returned to the airplane, wearing my spotted shirt and smiling.

Over the next few weeks, we had plenty of lengthy phone conversations, and as luck would have it, Charlie had business in Phoenix the following month. I just happened to have time off; otherwise, our phone friendship would likely have fizzled with time. His trip was filled with meetings, but there was plenty of time to get together for lunches and dinners. I like "meal dates." They are good testing grounds to see what kind of manners a man has. You find out if he is a control freak or talks with his mouth full and, more importantly, how he treats the waiters. Charlie always asked where I would like to sit, offered to pull out the chair, never talked with his mouth full, and was kind to everyone from the maître d' to the busboys. Perfect score. He had passed the meal test, so now it was time to take the next giant step. Golf. I can tell a lot about a person by watching him participate in a sport. Golf is a mental game. So, on his next visit he brought his sticks, and I must say he passed the second test with flying colors. We laughed more than hit the ball. Another perfect score.

The following month, I took a few days off to see Charlie and to golf on his turf. He had a home on Lake Chelan, which is about a three-hour drive northeast of Seattle. Driving all alone in a car with someone you hardly know can be challenging. It's hard even with someone you do know. Nevertheless, we chitchatted non-stop, and the hours seemed to fly by. It was the beginning of summer, perfect outdoor weather. When we weren't golfing or gambling, we were catching a good suntan while boating on the largest natural lake in the United States. Lake Chelan is pristine, and the nearby town is charming, its small markets filled with local fresh fruits, homemade breads, and quaint bookstores. Since Charlie lived nearby, we didn't have to deal with the awkwardness of checking into a hotel and wondering if we should get two rooms or share a room.

During our one-year relationship, I met Charlie in San Francisco, we visited Lake Chelan a few times during the summer months, and we spent time together when business brought him back to town. Charlie was fun and low key. We always had great times together; it was like being on a mini-vacation when we were together, which made it even more difficult when our playtime was over, and I had to return to work. And, once again, spending hours traveling across the country, missing flights, juggling schedules, leaving my dogs, as well as trying to meet my own personal financial goals took their toll.

Even though I was still young, I had spent 13 long years in the nut house. I had a personal goal to be debt free, which meant I needed to "make hay while the sun shined," as my grandmother used to say. I wanted to own my home free and clear. That was freedom to me. Debt was the Devil's handcuffs that kept me from doing whatever I wanted with my life. I was raised that if I had a roof over my head, the world could fall apart, but my world would not. So, in my mind, I first and foremost needed to get rid of the handcuffs before I could perfect my golf game.

I would have continued seeing Charlie, and perhaps we could have made our geographically undesirable relationship work, but at just about that time, a friend introduced me to a geographically desirable man: Larry. Larry didn't golf. Looking back, I can see that was a sure sign. But we did have dogs in common, and that was a big hit with me, at the time. Larry, the local guy, loved his dogs, and he seemed to love mine too. He had been working within the airline industry in one way or another for most of his life and knew firsthand the drama that accompanies travel. I dated both men for a few months, knowing I would soon have to choose one. Charlie and I never talked about being exclusive, but I knew it was about time for that talk. I was tired of traveling and not having any time to myself and, believe it or not, I was not good at complaining or communicating my needs, so I chose the easy route and stopped seeing Charlie. Choosing Larry seemed to make more sense. I wasn't looking for a husband, although Charlie would have been a great candidate. I was more interested in paying off my house so I wouldn't have to think about passing out nuts with one hand while pushing a walker with the other. I was trying to be logical and independent. Both of these men were fun to spend time with, but it when it came time to make a choice, I chose the geographically desirable man. Not because he was the best candidate for a date, or husband for that matter. I chose Larry because he was easy; he was local. Local Larry could take care of my dogs when I was at work and play a substitute cabbie every now and then. Shallow Stew, I know, and believe me, I did pay the price.

To those of you wondering what happened in my next relationship … well, I'll just say this: "Hindsight is 20/20." You haven't heard the last of Local Larry.

Road Sex

OK, I briefly mentioned that Pilots might spread rumors about Stewardesses; everyone knows Pilots have time on their hands. Rumors or fact? How will one ever know?

Passengers who wonder what really goes on in the cockpit between Pilots and Stews are curious and imaginative. ("Cock-pit": how appropriate.) They wonder if they mix, mingle, co-min-gle, and, perhaps, "Swingle!" They conjure up visions and dirty images of lurid affairs in this said "cockpit," as the curtain is pulled, the door is quietly opened, and the Slutty Stews slither in. Autopilot takes over as the entire crew strips off their uniforms, the heat-seeking missiles come out to play, and the joysticks get sticky. Susie Stew suddenly turns into Nasty Nanci, and the orgy begins. Buck-naked, they feed one another rich caviar and steak tartare, while sipping French champagne stolen from First Class. (Caviar? First Class? What an imagination! Leslie Nielsen and the crews of "Airplane 1-27" have provided salacious fodder for those images.)

I'll admit that some late-night overnight parties do still go on after the bars close down, but I have yet to get naked in a group on or off the airplane, or be fed anything but deep-fried cheese or stale chips and salsa from the bar menu. The infamous Pea Party pretty much put a damper on knocking back one too many, stay-ing up past curfew, and dancing on tabletops on overnights. Fly-ing with "cocktail flu" is pretty much a thing of the past, autopilot or not, but many great stories are floating around out there. Sure, there were Pilots who would stand behind the Stew and give her a penetrating shoulder massage to send that "Welcome, We're

Still the Friendly Skies" image to passengers as they boarded. A shoulder massage ... what a treat, and something I used to look forward to, until one time, the Pilot's wooden little pants-puppet hit me mid-bun. I must say it certainly added an element of surprise, and I was almost flattered, until a couple of weeks later, when I overheard some of the other girls talking about the same Pilot and his wandering pocket pal, "Woody," knocking at their back door too! Evidently, I wasn't the only backyard Woody liked to play in. Pilots can be so slutty.

Dating an airline person can be much easier than dating a non-airline person, for many reasons. Airline people understand airline lingo; how to bid for a schedule, trade days, and commute; the mechanics of "non-rev" travel; and the importance of detoxing and being left alone. They have their own particular hope list and work in the same chaotic environment; they understand what living in hotel hell is like. They know to always expect the unexpected. They know about weather delays, re-routes, bad food, and no food. They know that after a 12-hour day, you don't always get to go home. They understand waiting outside the airport in a snowstorm for 30 minutes, while waiting for the hotel van that may or may not come. They've made the series of calls to the hotel night receptionist asking sheepishly, "Where is our van?" They get the same, expected pat answer as we do: "It's on its way." They've taken the hotel elevator up to the 14th floor, subconsciously thinking, "Please make this key work." They've dragged their tired body and bags back down to the lobby to wait in line for another key, only to return to find that the second key doesn't work either. They understand that it's 35 degrees outside and that their heating unit blows only freezing cold air at 2 a.m., not exactly the time you want to call a strange hotel mechanic up to "tweak your unit," so to speak.

Pilots understand what flying through time zones does to a person's bodily functions—or, shall I say, lack thereof. They understand why a person may need to sleep until 4 p.m. the next day. They understand not to ask their girlfriend what time it is, because neither person really cares. They understand that the first things a Stew does when she finally gets home are grab a bottle of wine, fill the tub with bubbles, light a candle, and lock the door. (Or is it grab a bottle of wine, lock the door, fill the tub with bubbles, and light a candle?)

I guess someone more qualified—someone who was actually married to, or has dated, a Pilot—could write a full manual on the good, bad, and ugly. But the only real people seriously interested would be Pilots and Stewardesses, and they are already well aware of the positives and pitfalls. I am certain though, of the top two reasons Pilots and Stews make a perfect fit:

They're away from home a lot.

They're away from home a lot.

What a Stew really wants when she comes home is to not have to explain her mood. It's relatively simple. If no one is home, there is no explaining to do! From reading this book, you already know that having a relationship with an airline person certainly has its idiosyncrasies. Training a new mate that is a non-airline person is, again, time consuming and exhausting for both involved. Perhaps that's one reason some Pilot/Stew relationships work, although they can also be short-lived. (Not that that's a bad thing!) The training period is very short; they both work in the same wacky world and learn to endure crazy, out-of-control environments and schedules. They walk the walk; they fly the sky! They share a multitude of common denominators, which helps them to understand one another without having to talk it through. The no-talking rule: Priceless. If for some reason it doesn't work out, it's pretty easy to trade him in for another. The air is filled with single (and married) Pilots looking for love.

Another reason it may be easier to date airline employees is that they can schedule around each other's needs when it comes to taking care of the kids, family pets, and such. Unfortunately, one of the top needs of Pilots is sex when they arrive home. The number one item on their honey-do wish list is "Honey, Do Me." As I said, it *is* a WISH LIST, and you must know by now, that doesn't fly! Good grief, they want sex before they come home; that alone will most certainly ruffle a few Stew feathers!

Now, I am fairly sure that some percentage of Stews don't mind if their Pilot boyfriends and/or husbands have "Road Sex." (The definition of "Road Sex" is just that: sex on the road. Sex while they are away from home. It's not literally sex on the road; picking gravel out of a knee is really painful, and, besides, there is nothing to hold onto. Plus, someone might get run over!) Anyway, I am certain a few tired Stews would rather their men have road sex; that takes one item off the Stews' own "to-do" list when they get home.

On a more serious note, the majority of Stews are monogamous. It's hard enough for us to keep one man happy. ☺

Stew Dos

Bravo! You have successfully navigated the minefields of on-board manners, flirting, preliminary equipment check, suave flirtation, cool departure, and reasonable behavior. You've had your first, second, or even third date without blowing it by breaking the rules. Perhaps you've been lucky enough to join her on an overnight of your own ... at her place, of course. Lucky you! Now, let's see if your luck continues; this is where the game heats up and another set of plays unfold.

With any recipe, it is up to the chef to add a pinch of this or a pinch of that in order to put his signature on the dish. If you want an award-winning relationship, tenderizing is not an option; it is a must. Without it, your relationship will turn out to be as tough as buffalo hide. Sweeten the pot with some of the confections below.

Wine Is the #1 Winner

A nice bottle of her favorite wine is always a winner when you're welcoming her home. Make that two bottles. (If your relationship is such that you have a key to her casa, leave the bottles in her refrigerator; if not, just bring a nice bottle with you when you pick her up for your next date.) She's been listening to whiners all day long; it is her "time to wine" now. Insider tip: If you cannot find her favorite bottle of wine at the liquor store, don't feel bad; ANY wine will do in a pinch. Most grocery stores will give a 10 percent discount when you buy six bottles. If you didn't know that before, you do now. That little tidbit of information will save you a bundle.

Snacks

When she gives you the key to the kingdom (let's think positive, shall we?), go ahead and put a few goodies in her refrigerator for her to find when she gets home. Ideas include fresh fruit and brie—something that doesn't take a lot of preparation and that compliments the wine. You don't have to do this always, just when you know she has had a particularly difficult day. A little kindness goes a long way when a girl has had a bad day.

Know When to Flower

Every now and then, it's thoughtful to indulge her with a single bud or a bouquet of flowers. For outdoor, minimalist types, fresh-picked flowers will be just fine. It's the thought that counts. Several things dictate whether you should buy a single flower, a bouquet, or no flowers at all. Again, keep in mind that every Stew is different. If she's going to be home for only a day or two, there is no need to spend money on a bouquet when she will not be there to enjoy it. Walking in the front door to find a withering, dead bouquet is too reminiscent of how a Stewardess feels after a road trip: dried, wilted, and in dire need of nurturing. (I put my flowers in the refrigerator if I am going to be gone for a day or two, and I cut the ends off every other day, which helps to keep them fresher longer.)

K. I. S. S.

Every now and then, leave a card or note on her door to welcome her home. The card doesn't have to be a Hallmark card; something handmade is just as appreciated and easy to make. Dress it up by adding a big chocolate kiss or her favorite treat for a little energy boost. Keep the note simple by saying something like, "Thinking of You" or "Glad You're Home." Shy away from sayings that tell her what to do such as "Call Me." She's been told what, when, and how to do things since she left, and when she finally arrives home, well, it might just be the straw that broke the camel's back. Play it safe. Leave candy and a "Sweets for my Sweet" note, and leave it at that.

Spa'h

If you can afford to treat her to a spa facial or massage, wonderful. If not, offer a foot rub or back massage at home. If you catch her in a moment of weakness, she may just accept the home spa'h. If that is the case, pick up some nice scented oils at your local body shop. If things get hot and heavy, you're in the heat of the moment, and you haven't pre-planned, go ahead and use Crisco or whatever oil is in the house. Do not use motor oil. It works just fine, but the stains will never come out. (FYI: Guys, "body shop" does not mean the local auto-repair shop. The correct Body Shop to go to is a girlie shop with lotions and potions. If you aren't sure what oils to buy, ask the counter girls; they are always very helpful when men come in to purchase something.

Have a nice hot bath with bubbles waiting for her and a few candles lit to set the mood. Who knows? She may just decide there's room in the tub for two. Just don't expect sex. Not that you won't get any, but just don't expect it.

Vacations

Plan a vacation and actually pay for tickets. I recommend flying on another airline, so she can be anonymous and not feel as if she should be handing out peanuts, helping to clean up, or discussing work in any fashion. It can really put a damper on the holiday mood. Besides, it wouldn't be a good idea to join the mile-high club on her own airline.

Emotional Support

Support her when she calls in sick, even if she is not. Everyone has "sick of it days," and there is a specific eye infection that goes around in the Stewardess pool. Pink eye is a highly contagious disease that Stewardesses get. A lot. It's when they can't see going to work. It's either that, or they may start inflicting wounds on themselves. Stewardesses do not get holidays off with pay, or any three-day weekends. Ever. They typically work through the "holi-daze," and all too often, they get re-routed and miss the family festivities altogether. So, let her have her pink eye days ... with support.

Visitation Hours

Stews have strict visitation hours. Don't take it personally. She may not want to see herself when she gets home, fearing the "Scary Stew" may appear! Be patient and wait for her call. Do not show up unannounced unless you want to drop off a bag of groceries and a bottle of vino. After you ring her doorbell, run.

Wine to Unwind

For some reason, wine is a cure-all. Garlic may be known in the homeopathic world to help with arthritis and inflammation, but when a Stew gets home, the best remedy to unwind is wine. Always double check that a nice white wine is chilling in the fridge or that a red is in the cabinet. Hopefully you know by now her drink of choice. Might I recommend at least two bottles? It's important to have a back-up, just in case a glass is accidently dropped or kicked over.

You'll also want to get a box of bendable straws. Sometimes, I find it best to lie down and drink, as there is less opportunity to stumble and fall. Truth is, a Stew can never have enough wine in the house. Stock up.

Therapy Pets

Pets run a close second to wine as far as helping a Stew unwind. The combination of both is the #1 cure-all. If she has pets, love them as if they were your own. If you do not love animals or perhaps you are allergic, you should probably get ready to make a few changes in your life: Learn to love her pets, and get your shots on a regular basis if you need to. Otherwise, make another airplane reservation and begin the search all over. Next time, before you plan the first date, be sure to ask the new Stew if she has pets.

If you want to stick with the Stew you've got, volunteer to feed, water, and pet her pet(s). Most Stews keep pets for peace of mind. Pets love to greet their master at the door, wet noses and tails wagging. (Yes, the female population is well aware that men have wet noses and wagging tails too, but when a Stew walks through her front door, animals rule.)

Pets don't criticize or make judgments. They don't bark, "You drink too much" or "You sleep too late." Their love is unconditional; they don't mind if she walks straight into the bedroom and goes comatose or opens a bottle of wine and sips out of a bendable straw. They don't mind if she is a "slouch on the couch" with a big bag of Fritos and jalapeño cheese dip, as long as she shares a bit. Whether it's bedtime or booze time, pets easily adapt to whatever her mood might be. They don't care if their master takes a shower or combs her hair. They never tell her that her breath is bad or that she needs to brush her teeth. There isn't any dialogue whatsoever. Pets are the perfect mates. A little wet kiss and a pat on the head, and they're happy campers. It is of the utmost importance that a Stew feels her pets are left in good hands while she is away, and if a potential date genuinely offers to take care of her pets, he's a shoo-in. Pets are great for therapy and much less expensive than going to seek professional counsel every day. It's pretty simple: You take care of her pets, and she'll take care of you. As soon as she wakes up and has a cup of coffee, she'll give you a call.

Stew Taboos

1. Don't expect sex. Not even cadaver sex. She may be dead tired when she gets home, but sex—any sex in any shape or form—is out of the question. What she needs is to lie down. Alone. A more thoughtful idea: If you really care for her and you're concerned that she may have "passed on to the other side," simply place a mirror just under her nose every now and then; if it fogs up, she is still alive. Still, do not attempt to have sex.

2. Don't call her on her overnight and go on and on about what a great day you had at the golf course, glistening lake, or backyard barbecue with all your friends. Hearing stuff like that will only make her feel bad. For one, she is stuck in "Hotel Hell", otherwise known as "Solitary Confinement/Lock Down." She is at work; there are no lakes to go swimming in and no water-skiing with friends, and there is absolutely no drinking beer or any other adult beverage within eight hours of her next assignment. On an early-morning check-in, she may be waking up to a 1 a.m. reveille from the much-hated hotel alarm clock. And then she will shower, shampoo, and haul her draggin' behind down to the hotel lobby, mentally preparing herself for another full day of passengers saying, "You look tired," while envisioning her loved ones tucked in and sleeping off a full day of water-skiing and a belly full of potato chips and hot dogs. Another reason she'll feel bad is that she feels bad you are having a good time … without her.

3. If you live together, do not leave the laundry for her to do when she gets home. She has been cleaning up the airplanes for days. Please, do not leave dirty dishes, or dirty laundry, lying about. Hide it if you have to and wait until she's in a better mood before you give her your lame excuse as to why you didn't have time to take care of it. Stuff the laundry under the bed and the dishes in the dishwasher and cabinets, if you must.

4. Whether you pick her up from the airport or are waiting for her at home, when she walks through the door after her trip, don't get mad when she gives the cats and dogs love before you get yours. It doesn't mean she loves them more than she loves you. Animals cannot contain their feelings of excitement when the missing link walks through the door, and they have no idea of a pecking order. Be an adult; let Tigger and Muffin get a hug or two. You'll get yours after she has had time to unwind and detox with a nice long nap or hot bath—and the bath is waiting for her, right?

5. Don't be home when she arrives, unless you've pre-planned that scenario. (This way, you'll never get your feelings hurt if she goes for the "pooch smooch" before you.) It's for your own good. Stews are in a "limbonic" state, flying around in outer space for days; it's going to take a much different kind of space in order for her to be grounded and "get back to earth." She's been in crazy orbit; it'll be a while before you see "Abby Normal" again. I recommend that you keep your distance, unless you'd like to take part in an exorcism.

6. Don't make plans with friends or plans to go out the same night she arrives, unless you have asked permission and received approval ahead of time. Stews are bombarded with needy people day in and day out, and they need to find a quiet place to unwind. Don't be surprised if she has changed her mind by the time she gets home. Mood swings are a part of her profile.

7. Keep out of her way when she's preparing to leave for work. The energy force of a Stewardess changes as soon as she starts to plan and pack for the next trip away from home. Animals pick up on it. It's a good idea to stay out of her way when she is "putting on her game face." Much like football or baseball players, Stews need to get mentally prepared for the freakin' flying game. They have their own checklist, packing, and timing down to a science. They know exactly when they need to walk out the door, and there is absolutely no time for error or misplaced keys. They've got to gear up for the challenging days ahead, and at this point, no one can assist. Just get out of her way. I recommend running an errand or going to the gym. More squabbles have happened just before takeoff and right after arrival than at any other time spent together. This is time to give her some space. I know it is hard for anyone to be around me during my pre-flight checklist. My dogs go to the corner and pout as soon as they see me getting my "clown suit" out of the closet. I also had a cat that would crawl up onto my suitcase and use it as a kitty litter box. Now, there's a diversion!

8. Never ask her how her day was; you might just get your head bitten off. A better choice is, "Honey, I'm glad you're home" and leave it at that. Depending on her response, you'll know how her day went. If it was bad, most likely she will go directly to the refrigerator or wine cabinet, and she and Miss Chardonnay will step into the next room, close the door, and call a sister Stew to spew. Let her go. She is doing you a favor. Only another Stew can relate to the stories that need to be told: the stories of "The Freakin' Fliers."

9. Do not answer her phone. "The company" can call 24 hours a day. If an untrained, unassuming, non-airline person answers her phone and hears a person on the other end ask, "Hi, is Susie Stew home?" and then that someone happens to say, "Golly sure, just a minute," she

is cooked. Even if she's walking out the door for a fully paid, non-refundable two-week Polynesian vacation, she cannot turn down whatever trip they have to offer. Sure, she can still go on the vacation, but while she's there, it might be a good idea for her to begin her job search, since she'll be looking for another position upon her return. Be guaranteed the message light at home will be blinking, and there will be a final send-off from her snooper-visor asking her to return her manual and identification badge. No two-week notice. No severance pay. So put a star by this one, and make sure it is on your "Don't Ever, Ever Do List!"

10. If you are thinking of asking her for her hand, a word of advice: Do not ask her on the airplane. This is a "#1 NO NO!" You wouldn't go to a girl's office to ask her for her hand, and you really shouldn't propose to a Stew at her place of work. If you feel you need to be up in the air, or somewhere she can't escape, try a hot air balloon. It's much more romantic. Besides, if you ask her while she is working, the ring might not slip over the latex glove—or, worse yet—she may get re-routed.

Fly Straight, Boys

Perhaps I shouldn't share this bit of information, but honesty is always the best policy—most of the time. For those of you who may think, "When the cat is away, the mice will play," think again. When you least expect it, Susie Stew may just be re-routed, causing her schedule to change. Most of the time, a schedule change means she will be assigned additional routes and she will be delayed in getting home; then again, on a rare occasion, she might be released early. I doubt that I need to continue explaining the flow of thoughts and actions that follow. So, fly straight, boys; these girls might pick up a trip or give it away, and their schedules are never etched in stone. If for some reason they feel the need to do a little investigative "undercover" work and only pretend to leave town, they can. You'll never know if she's been cleared for departure, or if she's circled back around for a closer look.

Joe Re-Route

Sometimes, I lie. It's not something I *want* to do; it's something I *must* do. Call me a bad Stew? I call it self-preservation. I sometimes lie and tell people that I'm at work, but I'm not. I tell harmless little fibs because I don't have the energy to explain why I don't want to leave my house and go out in public, where there are people, cars, and well—people. I don't lie all the time, just when I know that I'm near the "going postal point" and it's in everyone's best interest that I stay behind closed doors. Alone.

I once got caught in my little white lie. A guy I was seeing for a couple of months didn't quite understand the seriousness of my number one dating rule: "If you don't bother to call, don't bother to knock." (Needless to say, he was having a hard time with initial training.) I had been out working for five days straight. When I got home, I just wanted to curl up with the dogs and go to sleep like Juliet, only without my Romeo. I called Joe from the airport as I was headed for my car (airport ambience is a must when making the call) to tell him I had been re-routed and was not going to be coming home that evening; I would call him the next day. Then, I drove straight home and hopped in bed instead.

Well, Joe, being new and all goo-goo eyed and infatuated with dating a Stew, thought it would be a good idea to use my hidden key and put a bouquet of sun flowers and an "I miss you" card on the nightstand since I would be away from home an additional night. (Not.) Little did he know I was already in snooze land with my pepper spray pal under my pillow and my two dogs sleeping nearby. I was tired with a capital T. I felt like Superman drained by kryptonite. I was dead to the world, and my two 85-pound pups were snoring to beat the band, so loud I guess none of us heard Joe come in the door—until it was too late. As he switched on the bedroom light, my two best friends and bodyguards, Ike and Tina, flew off the bed. I grabbed the pepper spray and was just about to hit the top lever, when I realized it was just Joe. Long story short: Joe's jeans were a bit ripped, but ripped jeans are cool; our relationship was not so cool, nor was it worth mending.

The moral of the story is that we Stews have the ability to, let's say, "massage" the truth if we feel the need. I could just as easily have met a girlfriend for a glass of wine, or driven to Joe's house to surprise him—or I could have told the truth: that I was beat and needed some "me time." Joe was seriously insecure and needy and couldn't understand why I wouldn't want to see him the minute I returned from a trip. He missed me; why didn't I miss him? He had a hard time giving me space. He smothered me. That's why I had to lie and that is why I told him, "Bye-bye."

I don't lie to get out of family functions like my parents' 50th anniversary party, but I have lied to get out of attending recreational functions like center seats at the Suns' basketball game and back-stage passes to the Rolling Stones. Functions with auditoriums filled with loud screaming or people drinking, or functions like movies where people are sitting in little rows, sharing armrests with strangers. I've always wondered why I never hear anyone complaining about the cramped seating at movie theaters; maybe it's because people are going to be entertained—or maybe it's because they can get up and leave whenever they want. They are not trapped and locked inside. They have control.

Whatever the reason, I have to lie. I do it to keep my sanity. After all, I have a reputation to live up to: a happy Stew.

Weather Concerns

Weather plays a large role in the life of a Stewardess. It is constantly changing, it is out of control, and it can certainly cause unexpected turbulence at the most inopportune time. Here are some of the things a Stewardess must weather on a daily basis, weather being just one of many:

1. Weather she remembered to set her alarm.

2. Weather or not she'll wake up when her alarm goes off.

3. Weather or not her baby-sitter is going to call in sick.

5. Weather or not her kitty used her luggage as a cat box—again.

5. Weather or not she forgot her credit card or money at home.

6. Weather or not her file will contain a "Come See Me" note from her supervisor.

7. Weather or not she'll be flying with an ex-boyfriend.

8. Weather or not she'll be flying with an ex-sister-in-law.

9. Weather or not the flight is going to take off on time.

10. Weather or not the flight is going to land on time.

11. Weather or not she'll get re-routed and have to spend an additional night away from home.

12. Weather or not her passengers will be naughty.

13. Weather or not there will be an emergency evacuation.

14. Weather or not a terrorist is going to light his underwear on fire.

15. Weather or not there is going to be a security breach at the airport.

16. Weather or not her crew will be compatible.

17. Weather or not a creepy freak with more peanuts in his mouth than teeth will try to hit on her.

18. Weather or not the hotel van will be waiting.

19. Weather or not the hotel will have a room available.

20. Weather or not the hotel will have heat and hot running water.

21. Weather or not she'll be the lucky one chosen for the Pea Party.

22. Weather or not she has enough gas to make it home at 4 a.m.

23. Weather or not she will sleep until 4 p.m. the following day.

24. Weather or not her "honey bear" kept the house clean and remembered to do the "honey-do" list that she taped to the refrigerator.

25. Weather or not she can sneak into the house without waking everyone.

The list of weather delays is infinite, and more often than not, delays affect her home life. One thing is for certain: A Stewardess needs a man who knows when it's time to have dinner on the table and a nice bottle of wine, or when it's time for the kids to go to grandma's house for the night. She needs a man that is psychic. She needs a mind reader. Because the majority of times when she finally reaches *her* final destination, she's just too plane tired to tell him what she wants. Peace and quiet; that's a given, and she needs space because she's been locked up in an airtight capsule during the day and a hotel cell at night—which brings me to my next subject...

Hotel Hell

What the hell is it? For those of you who have traveled extensively, there is no need for explanation. For those who have been lucky enough to keep their feet on solid ground, here are a few examples of Hotel Hell:

- ✔ It's waiting for a hotel van in the middle of an unexpected blizzard without a coat.

- ✔ It's finding that there isn't room at the Inn, so you're shuttled to another hotel, another 30 minutes away.

- ✔ It's when your room card doesn't work, so you have to drag your bags (yes, the ones under your eyes, too) and your tired behind down the corridors to the elevators and back to the front desk to be assigned yet another card ... that doesn't work, either.

- ✔ It's when your toilet overflows at 2 a.m. and you've been told the hotel is at full capacity.

- ✔ It's when you find out the next morning the hotel clerk was a jerk and lied to you about the hotel being full.

- ✔ It's when Housekeeping knocks on doors to deliver room service and vacuums the hallways at 6 a.m. local (3 a.m. your time), when you just arrived at midnight.

- ✔ It's stuffing towels under your doorway to help muffle the noise of vending and ice machines and elevators being used throughout your stay.

✔ It's workmen jack hammering the concrete walkway in front of your room at dawn because the hotel's water pipes have frozen.

✔ It's not being able to figure out how to turn the alarm on or off.

✔ It's people leaving their television on loud when they check out.

✔ It's the people in the room next to you having monkey sex.

✔ It's listening to the headboard bang on the wall throughout the night.

✔ It's throwing back the bed cover to find that the sheets haven't been changed.

✔ It's finding "funny looking" hair in the bathtub.

✔ It's getting ready for bed and realizing you forgot your toothbrush.

✔ It's brushing your teeth with hemorrhoid cream, thinking it was toothpaste.

✔ It's dreaming that you are home, only to wake up and you're not.

✔ It's waking up to use the restroom and walking straight into a wall.

✔ It's miscalculating the different time zones; you're dressed and ready to go at 5 a.m., waiting in an empty lobby, until someone finally tells you that you're two hours early.

✔ It's riding in a hotel van at 3 a.m. with the lights on full bright, listening to morning people chirp about their lives … or anything for that matter.

✔ It's Easter Sunday with no place to eat except the hamburger hut two blocks away.

✔ It's finding a piece of a fingernail clipping in your Easter Burger.

✔ It's asking to speak to the manager and he shows up chewing his fingernail.

Hope Junkies

Why do so many Stews have gray hair and glasses? Sounds like a joke, right? Like why did the chicken cross the road? There has to be a good one-liner out there somewhere. Well, the fact of the matter is that some are hired that way (no joke), and some turned gray along the way. Most Stews with a hint of gray, however, have stayed in the industry for a good portion of their lives, hoping to find the silver lining.

Many factors certainly keep Stewardesses hoping for a better future in an industry that is so turbulent, unknown, and ever changing. Most of us grew up believing the life of a Stewardess was a position of poise, prestige, and respect, and perhaps if we all continue to lead by example, this tarnished airline industry will somehow find a way to shine someday. I myself am a simple Stew, constantly relying on hope. I am a hope junkie. I hope that my sense of humor will somehow get me through each day, or at least that the TSA security guards will get better looking. Is that too much for a Stew to hope for?

A Stew's daily hope list:

✔ She hopes she remembered to pack her top-three travel items: her birth-control pills; her nicotine patch; and Happy and Sleepy, her prescription pals.

✔ She hopes the electricity doesn't go off in the middle of the night, causing her to sleep through her wakeup call and miss her flight.

✔ She hopes she remembered the time change.

✔ She hopes her car starts at 3 a.m.

✔ She hopes she doesn't have a flat tire.

✔ She hopes she didn't leave her coffee on top of the car as she backs out of the garage.

✔ She hopes the airport entrance isn't shut down for construction.

✔ She hopes she didn't leave her identification badge at home.

✔ She hopes she doesn't have to sit outside in another sand storm while waiting for the airport shuttle.

✔ She hopes her underwire bra doesn't set off the airport security alarm, again.

✔ She hopes her schedule doesn't change for the worse.

✔ She hopes that when she arrives to the In Flight lounge, the snooper-visors won't be there to tell her that her nametag is on upside down and her shoes don't match, again.

✔ She hopes when she checks her employee box that there isn't a "Confidential" letter inside.

✔ She hopes her gate isn't the farthest one in the airport.

✔ She hopes the operations agents, Pilots, ground crews, passengers, and crew will just be nice to her.

✔ She hopes she won't open a can of Coke and have it explode in her face, again.

✔ She hopes she'll make it through the day without a toothache or migraine.

✔ She hopes she doesn't get a urinary tract infection on her six-hour flight.

✔ She hopes "Cousin Flo" doesn't come to visit during the emergency demonstrations.

✔ She hopes she doesn't have to stand in a snow blizzard or rain downpour while waiting for the hotel shuttle.

✔ She hopes the hotel linens won't look like they belong in a college dorm that must have sold their old rags on eBay.

✔ She hopes she and her crew don't get snowed in for five days in a cold hotel in the middle of nowhere.

✔ She hopes she can remember where she parked her car three days ago.

✔ She hopes she didn't leave her lights on.

✔ She hopes when she finally arrives home, her loved ones have read this book. If they have, she knows they will give her the space she needs and might possibly have her favorite bottle of wine, or any bottle for that matter, opened and waiting next to a nice hot bubbly bath just for one.

✔ She hopes they know she loves them.

✔ She hopes they know not to take anything she says or does personally; she's just plane tired.

✔ She hopes for a better tomorrow.

✔ She hopes that someday her ruby slippers really do work.

✔ She hopes that she doesn't get grilled with questions when she gets home.

✔ She hopes there's an extra bottle of wine chilled in the refrigerator.

Stage II: Mating Made Easy

The mating stage is a more involved, intimate phase where you may be invited to an "RON," otherwise known as a "regular over night" at her house. If you make it to this stage, I recommend buying a nice gym or travel bag because if you're the lucky guy she wants to share her morning Malt-O-Meal with, you'll be the one doing the traveling.

One of the drawbacks of dating a Flight Attendant is that she is constantly leaving home. Week after week, bags are packed; month after month, goodbyes are said, and off she goes into the wild blue yonder. Upon her return, there is one common thread shared by all Stews I know: They just want to sleep in their own bed. It's as simple as that. So, if you think you're ready for the next phase of "In Flight Dating," boys, gas up the car and pack your bag; this is where *you* hit the road.

The mating rituals of a Fly Girl are much more complicated than the simple dating rituals. When sleepovers enter into the relationship, the real games begin—games that include role-playing. Sounds like fun, right? Well, it can be, but you must be a good sport. A favorite game all Stews love to play is "Roll Over and Play My Errand Boy." This is where the "honey-do card" is introduced. You decide whether or not to accept the card. If you pass on this card, the game is o.v.e.r. So, if you are a gambling man and want badly enough to stay in this game, I suggest you "man up," play along, and accept your fate; it's payback time. The mission, if you choose to accept it, will look something like this:

1. Feed the cat.

2. Pick up a light bulb for the pool.

Looks simple enough, right? So, you accept the card and play along. You take the bait. How could it be so easy? You most certainly will get your well-deserved "honey-do" treat when she arrives later that night—to a kitty purring on its pillow and a pool lit up. (Be sure to take it upon yourself to do a few other sweet things that aren't on the list, like leaving a light on for her, turning on her favorite music … and need I remind you about the wine?)

Now that you've proven you're an excellent pet sitter, that you can change a light bulb all by yourself, that you can follow directions well, and that you can go above and beyond the simple list without being asked, it's time to move on to the next level. It's obvious you like games where treats are involved, so let's move on to a more exciting, challenging role. As your relationship grows, so does your "honey-do" list. If she leaves you a really long list, that, my good man, is a sign she's starting to fall for you.

When her car is in the shop, you'll need to be her chauffeur. If she doesn't have time to pick up her laundry at the cleaners, that chore will be added to the list; after all, it's just right around the corner. Your second level of honey-dos might look like this:

1. Provide "Princess Parking" (otherwise known as being her personal chauffeur to and from the airport).

2. Take her pet(s) to the vet and/or groomers.

3. Work on her laptop.

4. Be a wealth of information regarding minor plumbing issues, patching leaks in the roof, and general house and pool repairs.

5. Meet contractor(s) for work done on her residence.

6. Pick up lots of take-out dinners and movies.

7. Pick up her prescription at the drug store; after all, it's right around the corner as well.

8. Make a quick stop at BevMo! or your local discount beer, wine, and party shop.

For those that make it to the second level, don't be afraid of the list. Repetition is the key. The more lists you complete, the better you'll get at remembering what needs to be done, and someday—just maybe—if you make it to the next level, you won't even need a list.

Everyone has a different set of honey-dos, and you will be well rewarded *if* she returns and finds the list has been completed to her satisfaction, because all items on the list save money and time. More specifically, it will save money and time *for her*, and both are equally important and parallel in the life of a Stewardess.

Keep in mind that dating a Stew offers a man an upside and many perks beyond free flights and non-stop nuts, and that these more than balance out the honey-dos. Having a girlfriend that works out of town leaves a man plenty of time to continue going to football, baseball, and basketball games and drinking beer, working out, hanging out, and eating cold SpaghettiO's out of a can, if he likes. It can be a pretty good life for the right kind of "eat-out-of-a-can" man.

Living with a Stew definitely has its ups and downs—rewards and challenges like no other. During the mating phase, you learn about her many mood swings, how work affects her home life, and how sex goes from the back seat to taking a back seat and why. If you haven't figured it out by now, I'll let you in on a little Stew secret: The world does revolve … around her.

Boot Camp

Living with me is like being in boot camp. I am the Drill Sergeant. I know training has been difficult for the man I am seeing, but he must like it or he would have left, right? Good thing he has a great sense of humor. He has somehow lasted over six years, and I am so fortunate to have him in my life.

We were introduced through friends on a golf course. So, our first few months of dating included a lot of golf and giggles. If you haven't figured it out by now, I love golf. It is the perfect sport for me. It is outdoors in a beautiful setting, and the only time you hear someone scream is if they get a hole in one or hit the ball so far off course they have to yell, "Fore!" Other than that, it is a really quiet sport with lots of space.

In the beginning of our relationship, John couldn't figure out why I didn't want to go out to dinner and a movie. He thought it would be a nice treat, since I had been working for a few days. It took a long time for me to get him to understand that I was a bit phobic of places with little chairs and lots of people. After we started spending more time together off the course, he occasionally would bring over take-out dinner, knowing that it would almost take an act of God to get me out of my house.

Several times during the course of dinner, the phone would ring ... and ring ... and ring. He would wait a moment, look at me, and say, "Your phone is ringing." I would respond, "That's what it does." I seriously believe he was thinking that I wasn't answering because it was another man calling. As if I would have the energy to date two men at the same time.

John is a talker. He loves to talk on the phone and loves to talk as soon as I get home. He always feels like we need to talk and catch up. I'm not always the best listener, especially when I'm tired, so my girlfriend who introduced us, Nikki, had a genius idea and bought me a hand puppet to give to him. Now he has someone to talk to, and I can take my catnap. It works out perfectly. It's just finding what works for the both of you.

I think one of the reasons we have stayed together so long is that we have a mutual respect for each other's space. He has lived in different parts of the world, has traveled extensively, and knows all too well what jet lag does to a person. We have also learned to give a little. I know he needs to go to the movies in order to immerse himself in a story or plot that will take his mind off work, so every now and then, although I would rather stay home, I toss on a baseball cap and a blue jean coat and go to the movies. I may fall asleep eating my bon bons, but I think he appreciates the effort. In return, he understands that take-out and a DVD are more than enough to keep me happy after coming home from work. And when the phone rings, I know what he wants to say, but he doesn't. The little things are what truly matter.

When I am at home, I try not to let the outside world dictate what I do, because I am hobbled at work; from the time I check in to the time I leave, I am a captive. I am lucky I can work with friends at times and lucky to make new acquaintances; I am also lucky to have a job that still has some flexibility.

I could fill this book with stories I have heard while sitting on jump seats across the country, but as a practicing physician, I do have my code of ethics to uphold. I will tell you that all the Stews I've talked to—Toni of 20 years, Keri of 8 years, or a brand-new rookie—are all pretty much the same: tired. We work in a pressurized flying machine through migraines; our muscles are stressed and our rotator cuffs torn; and years of irregular sleeping and eating patterns, dealing with stressful situations during flights, and breathing recycled air lead to more work-related injuries and illnesses than any other 9 to 5 job on the ground.

I can tell you that the general-consensus #1 wish from all the Stews I have had conversations with over the years is this: space. If they can just get a little space when they come home and have a moment to catch their second breath, there is hope.

Part IV

The Final Approach

Stage III: Marry Me, Fly Free

For those who make it past the second stage and are considering moving onto the third stage—final approach—make sure you are emotionally and financially secure as a couple. This may sound a bit premature, but if you have any qualms about changing diapers; doing the shopping; mowing the lawn; making breakfast, lunch, and dinner for the kids; and sleeping alone, you may want to rethink your plan of action. Do it now, because once the honeymoon is over and the little swimmers are allowed to attach, the stork starts filling your home with little skippers, and the list of honey-dos grows and grows.

Let's engage in another imaginative exercise to help prepare you for what lies in the family forecast. Once you return from your Tahitian honeymoon cruise and decide to add one or more to the love nest, get ready for some unexpected turnovers. Not the sweet pastry kind with yummy cherry and apple filling, however; this turnover is where you get the role of mommy turned over to you. (There could be a nanny in your future.) Let's cut to the chase: Morning sickness, an aching back, and a big belly do not gel well with working in an environment where the air is filled with big bags, barf bags, food scents from around the world, and an aisle that's getting smaller every day. At some point, your Fly Girl will need to give her wings a rest. This equates to the end of free flights, insurance benefits, and a second income as well. Yes, when her are wings clipped, you'll no longer be considered "DINKs" (double income, no kids), and with less income and bills soaring sky high, it might be a good idea to start saving ahead of time. Look on the bright side: You'll be saving a ton of money on wine alone, so, then again, maybe you won't have to worry about losing that second income!

Let's just save some time and skip to the good part.

Nine months later, the baby bundle of joy has arrived. Mama Bird will eventually take flight and return to the front lines, leaving the two of you to bond. Leaving the love nest is not only natural but also important, for two reasons. First, the bills will be mounting, so the additional income will help to offset some of the financial pressure that accompanies starting a family. A second reason—and perhaps *her* most important reason—is she desperately needs a good night's sleep ... alone... and she's willing to take a chance in Hotel Hell. (At least she'll have a bathroom all to herself as well as time for a hot bath without a rubber ducky and a glass of wine or two ... or three.) After a few nights of 2 a.m. feedings, followed by dealing with a day or two of colic and diaper rash all by yourself, you'll know firsthand why that is so important.

Yes, returning to the front lines, she leaves you and the baby bundle behind. Packed in her overnight bag and replacing her old best friend Miss Chardonnay is her new best friend: the breast pump. Personally, I haven't given birth nor pumped, but I have listened to ladies who have gone through the pain of leaving an infant at home with a husband who heats up left-over pizza in the oven ... while it's still in the cardboard delivery box. I have overheard the mumbling coming through the lavatory door while she pumps and moans, "If he made more money, I wouldn't be here." Believe me, I know it's just a girl talking crazy because she hasn't had a cocktail in a while. Once the pumping is over and the wine starts flowing, life should be good again. Though the first few months of adjusting may be turbulent, once a routine is built and daddy gets used to wearing the pants and the apron all by himself, everything should get easier ... for her anyway.

Whether she's raising a newborn or a couple of teens, she's hoping to end her day in a beach-front hotel with room service, clean towels, a glass of wine or two, and her very own remote control. Well, as you can guess, it can become addictive. It won't be long before she'll be yearning for more nights away from home. While she's sipping her wine in a nice hot bath filled with bubbles, you'll be at home with Mr. Bubbles and more whining than one man can handle. You might even consider hiring a nanny.

Well, that's the perfect dream world for a Stew with children: nanny at home making fresh bread and pasta, beach-front hotel, room service on a quiet floor, and a remote with working batteries (just in case her own AA's run out of juice). That's what every Stew—married or not—dreams of. The reality is this: Very few Stews have the leisure of choosing an overnight with enough time to bake at the beach. Most Stews work for productivity and try to make as much money as possible, whether single or raising a family. Sure, sometimes she'll want to pick up a trip to anywhere just to get out of the house and to catch up on some lost shuteye, leaving you to run the circus alone. Other times, she'll beg to stay home, fearing her flights will be filled with crazed Super Bowl fans, bachelors, and bachelorettes going to Vegas to party hardy, or guys who have more peanuts in their mouths than teeth and who are telling her to smile.

More realistically, when the weary traveler finally returns home, she'll more than likely call ahead to alert every one of her arrival ... and mood. Whatever you do, don't start listing all the negative things that may have happened while she was away. Believe me when I say this: "As difficult a day as you may have had, in her eyes, you were still at home with your feet on the ground, and you didn't eat your meals two inches from a Porta-Potty."

Honey-Dos

More Honey-Dos? Seriously, men, you've been great sports up till now. Hang in there. You're just a few more Honey-Dos away from a home run-happy ending. By incorporating these next simple suggestions into your regimen, you are sure to be nominated for "Best Sport" or, perhaps, "Husband of the Year":

1. When she calls home, do yourself a favor; ask her if she needs some time alone. The last thing you'll want to do is be at home in a good mood when she walks through the front door in a bad mood. If she's had a hard day and needs time to detox, go to the gym or run errands for a couple of hours. (Otherwise, you might find yourself the matador and her the bull, and you'll be in a fight you'll never win. Leave before it gets bloody ugly.)

   If you have children, make prior arrangements with family or friends to drop off the kids for a sleepover or movie in case she's coming home a Zombie Stew. Maybe she'll just need a nap. Maybe she'll feel like cooking dinner. Maybe take-out is better. Or beer. Maybe just take the time to ask. It's pretty simple. Just ask. After a while, you'll get into a routine that works for both (or all) of you.

2. Cards and flowers still work. Every Stewardess loves to find a surprise flower on the counter or nightstand. Just don't spend a lot of money. She's paid an hourly wage and equates the cost of everything with how many hours she has to spend on the road away from home and family. To

get your money's worth, ask the florist which flowers stay fresh and last the longest. Be frugal, unless she makes a "cheap" comment about the single flower and the home-made card, and then simply tell her you were trying to be sensitive and save for a rainy day or vacation for the two of you. (Or baby #2?) Be creative and make something up.

3. Try to keep the house at least as neat as it was when she left. If you have the additional funds, might I suggest getting a part-time housekeeper? She doesn't have to be a live-in; maybe she can come once a month to do a thorough cleaning. Keeping house is a full-time job; being a Stewardess is full-time and a half.

4. A foot rub and a bottle of wine are always on the list. If you have had a tough day yourself and can't seem to muster up the energy to give her tired tootsies a rub, make sure your cabinet is stocked with twist-top wine and a few good DVDs.

5. Hold hands when you're crossing streets, and walk on the outside, nearest the curb, when walking down the sidewalk together. (Just a little, old-fashioned, romantic helpful hint.)

6. Last but not least, communication is key. When she is away, don't vent on the phone about all your troubles—unless you want to hear a dial tone. While she's dealing with delayed flights, lack of sleep, and bad food, you'll have to deal with the home and the family, financial, and personal problems. It can be overwhelming; try to remember to be friends first and foremost. Don't bombard her with issues as soon as she walks through the door; give her time to unwind. If not, get ready for an early 4th of July.

Living with a person that is absent part of every week traveling can be taxing for both parties. Sure, having the boys over to watch a game without having to ask permission may make you

"King of the Crib," but picking up the kids after school, dressing them and combing their hair for school pictures, and attending parent/teacher meetings all by your lonesome can be, well, lonesome. If family members, especially the kids' grandparents, can fill in every now and then, be sure to ask for their help.

Marriage Taboos

No need to beat around the bush. There are certain things a husband should know without having to learn them the hard way. Here are a few of my inside tips:

1. Do not expect sex. Husbands and children count the minutes until Mommy arrives. They miss her. They need her. They want her. They are oh so excited to see her—until they learn that "Mommy" has a need too. Mommy needs a stiffy. No, not Daddy's stiffy; the other kind. A tall one. A double. She has become a desperate housewife, desperate for a drink.

2. I repeat myself: Do not ask, "How was your trip?" When she returns home from the dirty bird, she may be in a very fragile state, and the simplest question or action may cause her to fly off the handle. Susie Stew may have walked out the door a few days ago, but it's Scary Stew when she returns, barely recognizable if it weren't for her nametag.

Sometimes, her flights are filled with courteous, nice people, and sometimes not; sometimes, the airplane cabin looks more like a zoo filled with crazed animals at feeding time. A Fly Girl's muscles ache at the end of the day, thanks to long hours spent stooping over as she asks passengers what they would like to drink; bending over to prepare the service; jerking, pulling, and tugging on heavy galley kits; contorting her body to fit between cramped rows of seats to clean up the airplane floor; and opening and closing heavy aircraft doors. This, however, is nothing compared to the mental fatigue of waiting on people all day long while being zipped up tight in "Sardine City."

If you make it to the final phase of marriage, you'll be well aware of the daily stress and drama a Stewardess endures. She works in a public environment where she must be the diplomatic ambassador 24-7, as all eyes are upon her, at all times. She is the original "Google Girl," expected to know everything about airline travel, food, lavatory availability, beverage menu, flight schedules and pricing, gates, baggage carousels, cabs, hotels, and much more. She wears the hats of a greeter, server, weather reporter, cleaner, cheerleader, and security guard, and she's expected to put her life on the line for 137 strangers and a cockpit crew if there's a flight disaster or terrorist attack. A Stewardess is always on high alert for in-flight drama and expected to make a split decision on whether it's best to pacify an unruly passenger or turn into Judo Jane. She can single handedly bring a 250-pound Grizzly Adams down to his knees at 35,000 feet all the while realizing if she makes a mistake, her job may be on the line.

Stews learn the hard way how to handle stressful passengers and situations on the airplanes. Their initial training does not prepare them to deal with smart-ass remarks and the daily demands of the public. She was taught to save someone's behind, not politically kiss it; that's on-the-job training. So, asking how her trip was might just be the trip cord that causes her head to spin ... around!

3. Do not have friends over for a pool party the day she arrives. Home is her sanctuary, away from crowds of noise and people. A Stew needs to have a safe place to go to, somewhere to totally be herself without having to worry about someone telling her to smile. This is her time to "detoxify." This particular type of detoxification does not omit alcohol; this type of detox usually mandates alcohol—a lot of it.

4. Do not have a list of things prepared for her to do when she arrives, unless you're prepared to sign divorce papers.

5. Do not have piles of dirty clothes in the laundry room, nor dirty dishes in the sink. Make an effort to keep the house clean.

6. Do not leave out bills that are past due. Pay them.

7. Do not drink the last bottle of wine. Ever.

8. Again, do not expect sex. If you remember only one thing, remember this one. Write it down on a sticky pad if you must.

The Institution

Here's a true story about the day in the life of a Married Stew.

The truth is I was institutionalized for a short while with Local Larry. I was single and very happy up until that point. The point where I said, "I do."

When Larry and I got married, he had a job. We both had jobs. Larry had a large house with a little yard; I had a little house with a large yard. We desperately needed a large yard to accommodate our four large dogs, so we chose to keep my house—for the dogs' sake. Shorty after the nuptials, Larry moved all his stuff into my little house and quit his job to start a new company. Oh sure, there were several reasons he decided to do all this, and believe me, at the time it all seemed to make sense.

This situation actually happens to quite a few newly married Stews. With a wife who earns a decent income, the new husband sees an opportunity to get out of his dead-end job, in the hopes of finding his dream job and ultimately giving the newlyweds a chance at a better life so that someday Susie Stew just might be able to give her trips away and have a better life too. But in the meantime, Susie Stew is the dedicated and sole breadwinner, who ends up working much harder than she did before she said, "I do."

With Larry's new venture, he gave his full attention to research and development, which meant extensive traveling and travel expenses—at my expense(s). Easy for him. So many of us Stewardesses stay in our job partly because it's flexible and we can pick up extra work. The key is to find a trip that meets your requirements, as far as the particulars of what time you check in at the airport, what time you are scheduled to arrive back home, and of course the pay. I went from working two or three days a week before Larry, to having five to six days off a month after Larry. I was away from home so much that I had to be careful when I walked through the back gate for fear that the dogs would take me for a stranger.

Before I was institutionalized, I wouldn't have dreamed of picking up extra work, especially over the Christmas rush. Any holiday travel is truly hellish. Airports are overflowing with anxious first-time flyers rethinking their choice of travel. Passengers are going on that once-a-year holiday cruise; they're anxious about meeting their mother- and father-in-law for the first time; they're bringing the kids to see Grandma and Grandpa; they're visiting a sick relative for the last time; there are a zillion other reasons why they choose to travel during this one particular week.

During boarding, family after family arrives late, holding babies and diaper bags, pleading in front of hundreds of on-time passengers for their Stewardess to inconvenience someone—any-one—so they may all sit together. Babies are crying, dogs are barking, and cell phones are left in the waiting area. Flights are late and cancelled due to weather and g'hod knows what. Airline employees around the world know that Christmas week is a good time to take a holiday from work and the crazy crowds, and to just stay home.

During Larry's and my first Christmas together, my new husband was in Los Angeles on monkey business—again. After all, he could now fly all over the country for free, and I guess since he felt *he* was "saving so much on airfare" he could afford a luxury car instead of economy and eat a steak dinner instead of a hamburger and fries. After all, a CEO has an image to maintain.

For my surprise Christmas gift, my thoughtful, unemployed husband planned a full-fare, non-refundable, wonderful ski vacation for three in Sun Valley. He was in Los Angeles (yes, again), and his nine-year-old son was home with me for the week; we were to join him in Sun Valley on the 22nd. I was well aware that he didn't have the funds to pay for "our family excursion," but I wasn't about to forfeit all the non-refundable fees, so…

This one particular holiday, the company was short handed and offering time-and-a-half pay to anyone who would pick up extra work. The morning of the 21st, I picked up a single day that was scheduled to get me home that evening in plenty of time to take care of last-minute details before leaving town. The next-door neighbors had four boys of their own and had agreed to watch my son for the day. I was scheduled to work three short flights and then "deadhead" home from Las Vegas to Phoenix. (Deadheading is when a crew member sits in a passenger seat instead of being a part of the working crew.) After I had flown my three legs and said goodbye to my crew, I walked up and out of the jetway at gate 28, proud that I'd been able to pick up a little extra income and juggle my "Wife Life" as well. It was a perfect fit—so it seemed.

As it happened, my last flight, to Phoenix, was going out of gate 8. As I walked up to the counter, the agent told me to run to gate 26 as a flight was leaving and I was needed immediately. I had forgotten my cell phone at home, so I asked to use the phone to call scheduling, as there must have been a mistake; I was not on reserve. The agent told me in a very matter-of-fact way that there was no time to call scheduling; there was a plane holding for me. Now, it is a well-known fact in the Stew world that a Stewardess cannot reject an assignment. If she does, that will be her last assignment. Ever. So, without a second thought, I hooked it back to gate 26 and boarded the flight, innocently assuming the aircraft was most certain to take me back to Phoenix somehow that night.

What happened next? I was wrong in my assumption. I must say, never in my wildest dreams would I have thought this would have been my destiny for the day; otherwise, I would never have made the call earlier. Forget about the full-fare flight I was supposed to take with my son to go on our first vacation as a family. Forget the six-night, seven-day stay at the Sun Valley Inn for Christmas. What I got for Christmas instead was a surprise that

I will never forget. I was given an extended stay in an Albuquerque hotel and was unable to make it back in time to give my diabetic dog, Tina, her insulin shots, nor pick up my son. My new husband had a new number, and I had no way of contacting him. When my flight landed in Albuquerque, it was 11 p.m. The neighbors had an unlisted number, which I didn't have with me, so I was unable to call them to explain my situation. I'm sure they thought the worst. I finally arrived in Phoenix the next morning at about 10 a.m.; unfortunately, our flight to Sun Valley had left an hour earlier.

I had already made previous arrangements with relatives in California to housesit for the week, and they were to arrive about noon. When they drove up, they found a welcoming committee of two. The house was a bit cramped, but it all worked out in the end. Larry went ahead and flew up to Sun Valley, expecting to see us at the airport. Surprise.

To add insult to injury, there were other financial costs to absorb:

- ✔ $1,325 for the cost of two non-refundable airline tickets.

- ✔ A $250 cancellation fee for the Inn, since the reservation wasn't cancelled 48 hours ahead of time. Larry decided to stay with friends. Good idea.

- ✔ A $400 vet bill.

What really put the frosting on the cake? The crew I flew with to Albuquerque informed me that the girl I'd replaced was a reserve based out of Oakland. In their haste, scheduling re-routed me to her flight assignment and routed her from Las Vegas to San Diego to overnight in Phoenix that night. Phoenix. Phoenix, Arizona. My home base. She could have stayed on her scheduled flight and overnighted in Albuquerque, and I could have easily flown the assignment they gave her, ending up at home just a few hours late. My Christmas calamity should never have happened.

For those of you interested in whatever happened to my wonderful husband, Local Larry, well, let's just say he was my first and last. The marriage lasted three long years. It seemed like a life sentence. If a girl gets one mistake in her lifetime, I guess Larry was mine.

When I went into the institution of marriage, I was sane. During my stay, I was destined to go crazy, and now I know why it's called "The Institution of Marriage." I'll take odds that when Frances went into the asylum, she was sane too; it was during her stint as a married woman that she went crazy. Environment is so important; if you hang around nuts long enough, you eventually go nuts yourself.

I learned a lot while I was "in"—things I wish I never knew, and things I will never forget. I did learn a dear lesson: Peace of mind and a simple life are of the utmost importance. That's why I had to break out of the "Inn-stitution." And that, my friends, is my very happy ending.

Evolution of the Stew

Stew Evolution

The Single Stewardess Faces the Brink of Extinction

More and more single Stewardesses fly off the single charts every single day, leaving fewer and fewer opportunities for another match made in heaven. Remember, it wasn't that long ago when the professional Sky Hostess was allowed to fly only if she was unmarried. Only single, beautiful chicks were chosen for this posh position, and once she flew down the road to matrimony, she had no choice but to retire, allowing a continuous fresh crop of available girls to enter the industry. Most glamour girls lasted only two to three years before flying the coop with some lucky man, giving another "SSF"—single, slender female—a chance to spread her wings and fly.

Not that I would ever question the written word, but this ingenious theory was obviously created by a man. It would almost lead one to believe that these game rules perhaps originated from a bunch of wealthy, married investment-type guys who became bored of flying around with their buddies shakin' n' makin' their own martinis and picking up after themselves. Maybe the first couriers were really their no-good sons who couldn't get passing grades in prep school, so Daddy decided to make 'em buck their bags and stuff to earn their keep. Maybe their boys were just spoiled rich brats, and it wasn't long before Daddy decided that replacing their lazy offspring with a few young, giddy broads to wait on them hand and foot and laugh at all their jokes would be much more fun than wondering if their sons were going to drain the liquor cabinet and drink all the good stuff, again. Maybe the first batches of Stewardesses were really handpicked secretaries for these guys, who figured it would be a great way to have an affair, out of the office. They could hire some old, fat broads to run the home office and take the young, sweet things on the road.

Maybe this whole scheme was put together in one late-night booze-up with the boys. Who else could have come up with some slightly prostitutional job description that would set the scene for young chicks flying in one door single, sappy, and slender but then being booted out the back door without a battle—or retirement—once they got old, fat, or both? Rich men, that's who. Men whose wives were beauty queens at one time, but after having a few babies, maybe they gained a little weight and didn't have time for their attention-starved husbands. To that, I say, "Bravo." This brilliant man-plan worked remarkably well—until women got a taste of having their own bank accounts and found out they could bring home the bacon and fry it up in the pan. Who needs a man? B'uh Bye, boys. Thanks, Mr. Rich Man. Hello, feminist movement. Sky Five!

Yes, as the years went by, the feminist movement freight-trained right on into the airline industry, making it harder and harder to ensure there'd be that fresh crop of new green girls every year. As the years passed, the airlines did start offering retirement packages to entice the older, wiser gals to hand in their aging wings, but these retirement packages have slowly become extinct, as has the concept of the single Stew. Nowadays, very few airlines offer any type of retirement package whatsoever, leading to a more well-preserved, aged-to-perfection (but not tough and crusty, I hope) kind of Stew that is sometimes referred to as "The Dinosaur."

And how does one get rid of a resurrected Dinosaur in the year 2011, you ask? Well, of course there are cold, cruel ways, though euthanization is certainly out. Stews have a bit more protection than they did in the early years; a company cannot kick its employees to the curb simply because they're not pleasing to the eye after all these years. Oh, they can reprimand them for not smiling; they can reprimand them for speaking their mind; they can suggest they wear support hose over their unsightly, bulging varicose veins. They just can't get rid of them because they are old or fat. Not anymore.

So, companies have come up with a more creative way to get rid of the "Old Glories": the ones who have weathered the storms; the ones who have spent most of their lives on the front lines battling the public, the companies, the unions, and now terrorists; the walking wounded. Now, there is a more humane way to get rid of the oldies but goodies: "Wear 'em down and work 'em to the bone … yard." Even though the work gets more physically and mentally demanding as the years go by, most Stews continue to make the best of every situation; they cope the best they can, and chill with a nice bottle of wine and a good man every now and then.

Nowadays, fewer and fewer Stews hand in their wings on their own accord, mainly due to economic reasons. Who's to say what the future will bring, but if the trend continues as it has over the past 60 years—and couple this trend with industry cutbacks on hiring and expansion—there is a great possibility of a mass extinction. It's pretty simple math: Fewer Stews hired due to economic reasons + Fewer Stews leaving + More male, married, older, and "other" Stews being hired + Stews getting married each year = Single Stew Extinction.

Stews are like commodities, only with great benefits. The sooner you make plans to land your own Fly Girl, the better. You had best get 'em while they're hot and spicy, boys. The best ones go fast. Everyone knows the numero-uno slogan "Marry Me, Fly Free," so if you're serious about landing a sweet young Stew, I suggest you get busy before they've all flown the coop.

Happy Trails

You now have a better perception of how and why dating a Stewardess is so rewarding, complex and completely different from dating any other woman in any other profession. You've been handed the basic tools to make your "Dream Stew" come true; you no longer have to just fantasize about her. Pandora's Box has finally been opened, and years and years of hidden secrets are now flying out for the entire world to hear! Keys to the unknown are at your fingertips and you now know secrets to a life most men only drool about. So wake up, have that second shot of espresso and dive right in to this intoxicating, new game.

Everyone in the business world knows the phrase "first to market," and dating a Stewardess is serious business and a fresh, delicious market I'm certain you'll enjoy. There is no need to call your broker; these rare gems don't trade on the market. This book may just be your best investment ever, and it's all you really need to be successful at landing the perfect Stew.

You've just been served an opportunity of a lifetime: free flights and more nuts than you can imagine. *How to Do a Stew* is a direct flight to exciting vacations, benefits galore, and much more. Fasten your seatbelts, men, and get ready to cook; there's a rare bird out there, and she won't stay single for long. Reserve your cheap ticket to anywhere today—before you hear the recording, "Sorry, Sir, all flights are full!"

In parting, I would like to remind you of two very, very important tidbits of advice I've already mentioned. The "Top Two Taboos" are these:

1. Never ask a Stewardess for her hand in matrimony while she is working on the airplane.

2. Never, ever, tell a Stewardess to "smile."

Happy trails to you … and may the best man win!

B'uh Bye!

☺